Derby County,

Champions at Last

A Diary of the Rams' Triumphant

1971-72 Season

Derby County,
Champions at Last

*A Diary of the Rams' Triumphant
1971-72 Season*

By David Moore

First published in Great Britain in 2012 by The Derby Books Publishing Company Limited, 3 The Parker Centre, Derby, DE21 4SZ.

ISBN 978-1-78091-072-2

Printed and bound by Copytech (UK) Limited, Peterborough.

Contents

Foreword

By Tony Bailey

I must admit to being surprised when David Moore asked me if I would supply a foreword to his book about Derby County's Championship winning season of 1971-72. After all, I wasn't exactly a household name during my time at the Baseball Ground but I was fortunate enough to play one First Division match for the Rams during that momentous season. As David said when we met, a lot of Derby supporters would have settled for that.

That single League appearance was against Don Revie's formidable Leeds United side at Elland Road on the afternoon of Monday 27 December 1971 and I suppose Brian Clough couldn't have arranged a more difficult baptism if he'd tried. In the run-up to the game it was obvious that Colin Todd would be unable to play because of a broken nose so the gaffer turned to me.

I had joined the Rams from Burton Albion in February 1970 after being spotted by Peter Taylor but with so many great players at the Baseball Ground it was always going to be extremely difficult to break into Brian Clough's wonderful team on a regular basis.

I eventually made my first team debut in a Texaco Cup match away at Dundee United in September 1971 playing alongside Terry Hennessey. We lost 3-2 but as Derby had won the first leg 6-2 we were all but certain to reach the next round anyway. Not that the manager was happy about the three late goals that we conceded after going 2-0 up – he made that pretty clear.

Three months later I was selected for the second leg of the Texaco Cup semi-final at Newcastle United's St James' Park. I was told an hour or so before the match that I was playing with the instructions to keep centre-forward Malcolm MacDonald quiet. There were 37,000 in the ground and they made it fairly obvious what they thought of me when I was booked for clattering into him but SuperMac soon got his own back by thumping me in the ribs.

A month later came that League debut at Elland Road. What a side they were. We were on a bad run away from home anyway but a full strength Leeds were far too strong for us that day. I didn't have a particularly good game and, to be honest, no one else did either but standing in for a great player like Todd was bound to be difficult. It all seemed a blur but I do remember getting booked for fouling centre-forward Mick Jones.

That turned out to be my one and only League appearance for Derby although I played in virtually every match for the reserves when we won the Central League the same season. In October 1973 Dave Mackay replaced Clough and the following January he decided to send me out on loan to Oldham. Three months later I joined them permanently for a fee of £6,000. Actually, it wasn't quite as permanent as I thought it was going to be because by the end of the year I was playing for Third Division Bury. Gigg Lane might not have been quite the same as the Baseball Ground but I had six enjoyable years there.

I first met David Moore when we played in the same cricket team in the 1960s and I remember he was Derby County mad even then. David's book brings back memories of that wonderful season when the Rams won the League title. It was a marvellous time for me. I have always regarded it as a privilege to be associated with so many great players and I still look back on it with a lot of affection.

That's why I'm happy to be associated with David's book. I hope you enjoy reading it as much as I've enjoyed talking to him about those long lost days at the Baseball Ground.

Acknowledgements

Firstly I would like to thank Tony Bailey for agreeing to provide a foreword for this book. I could tell what his relatively short time at the Baseball Ground meant to him when we had a chat recently and, hopefully, so can you after reading his contribution.

I have read and digested very many match reports from newspapers before penning my own versions but obviously I am particularly grateful to Gerald Mortimer and George Edwards of the Derby Evening Telegraph for their splendid work. The Ram, Derby County's newspaper style matchday programme of the 1971-72 season, has proved extremely useful too and I have included a few of the front covers in the book..

A full list of other sources is appended in the bibliography at the end of the book and I am grateful to all of them. Finally, I would particularly like to thank Steve Caron of DB Publishing for giving me the opportunity to put together this book about the Rams and also for giving me permission to use some photographs from earlier publications.

Seventy-two Seasons
& Still Waiting

When preparations for the 1971-72 season began, surely not even the most optimistic supporter expected Derby County to be crowned as champions the following May. Although the previous season had ended on a positive note, finishing the new one above the likes of Leeds, Liverpool and double winners Arsenal wasn't a realistic prospect, particularly as there had been so little transfer activity in the close season at the Baseball Ground.

Although Derby County had occasionally come close to winning the coveted First Division title since joining the Football League as one of the 12 founder members in 1888, they were still waiting to lift the trophy 83 years later.

A total of 11 seasons had been lost to the two World Wars and of the remaining 72 Derby had played 45 in the top flight including the first seven when the Football League consisted of a single division. All but two of the remaining 27 had been spent in the Second Division but there had been a couple during which the club had been forced to suffer the ignominy of competing in the Third Division North.

Derby finished third in Division 1 at the end of the 1893-94 season (by then the Football League had expanded to two divisions) and two years later were runners-up, four points behind champions Aston Villa. Hopes must have been high that they would go one better the following term but once again, despite the presence of the prolific Steve Bloomer, they had to settle for third place with Villa winning the title for the third time in four seasons, 11 points ahead of second placed Sheffield United.

It was a case of so near, so far in the FA Cup too. Derby reached the Final for the first time in April 1898 only to lose 3-1 to Nottingham Forest at Crystal Palace with Bloomer scoring the consolation goal. A year later they travelled to the capital for their second Final. This time the opponents were Sheffield United who went one better than Forest, winning 4-1. Boag's goal for Derby must have seemed almost as hollow as Bloomer's had been the previous April. Even worse was to come four years later when the Rams, under their first manager Harry Newbould, were thrashed 6-0 by Bury. It was a record score for an FA Cup Final at the time and remains so to this day.

Impatient supporters had to wait until the end of the 1911-12 season before their side won its first piece of silverware but, ironically, they had to be content with doing so as champions of the Second Division. They had been relegated for the first time in 1907 and it had taken them four seasons to return to the top flight. Sadly, they found themselves playing Second Division football again in the 1914-15 season but this time they bounced back straightaway and in doing so won their second trophy after finishing top.

By the late 1920s Derby County had become one of the most powerful clubs in the country and George Jobey's star-studded side ended the 1929-30 season as Division One runners-up for the second time, albeit 10 points adrift of champions Sheffield Wednesday, Although the Rams rarely finished outside the top six in the seasons leading up to the Second World War, the closest they came to winning the title was in 1935-36 but once again they had to be content with finishing second.

League football re-commenced in August 1946 after a seven-year hiatus. A few months earlier, of course, the Rams had won the FA Cup for the first time in their history on that legendary Saturday afternoon at Wembley Stadium. Hopes were high that Stuart McMillan's team might go on to lift the First Division trophy in the near future but, sadly, the wonderful side which included Carter and Doherty, arguably the best inside-forward pair in the country, soon began to break up.

Doherty played in just a handful of League games before moving to Huddersfield in December 1946 and in came Scottish international Billy Steel from Morton to replace him for a British record transfer fee. Carter moved to Hull City in March 1948 but although Derby finished the 1947-48 season in a highly respectable fourth place they had never been serious contenders for the title.

Exactly a year after Steel's arrival McMillan broke the British transfer record for the second time when he persuaded Johnny Morris to join the club from Manchester United. Morris was an instant success and Derby came even closer at the end of the 1948-49 season but in the end they had to settle for third place.

Hopes had been raised as early as the beginning of November after they had beaten Birmingham City and moved to the top of the table for the first time, one point clear of Portsmouth. Two weeks later the Rams moved further ahead after consecutive victories over their main rivals away at Newcastle and then at home to Pompey, Billy Steel scoring the only goal of the game. By the time Derby travelled to Stoke on 11 December they had opened up a three-point gap and were beginning to look like serious contenders for the title. Unfortunately they had an off day. The Potters won 4-2, and the following week Derby went down 3-1 at home to Manchester United.

Crucially, as it turned out, leading scorer Jackie Stamps had picked up an injury which was to keep him out of action for over two months and by the time of his next appearance at the end of February they had dropped to third place, five points behind leaders Portsmouth. The chance of winning the title for the first time in their history was fading fast. Four weeks later they had virtually disappeared altogether after losing 1-0 at Fratton Park, which left them eight points adrift of Portsmouth the eventual champions.

By the time Derby travelled to Stamford Bridge on 16 April the slump had gathered pace but an unexpected 3-0 victory that day followed by five wins and a draw from the last six fixtures propelled them to third place at the end of the season. In hindsight it was a highly creditable position but at the time it was hugely disappointing after being so far ahead at the halfway stage. Unfortunately, as supporters were to discover, it would be a very long time before they reached those dizzy heights again.

By the early 1950s a serious decline was beginning and the last thing on the supporters' minds was lifting the First Division trophy. The immediate priority for Derby was to preserve their place in the top flight but although relegation was avoided at the end of the 1951-52 season the slide was gathering pace and the inevitable drop to Division Two took place a year later.

No one was surprised when McMillan's threadbare squad continued to struggle, even in the second tier, and in November 1953 he was replaced as manager by Jack Barker, the Rams' ex-England international centre-half. It would have been a daunting task for the most accomplished manager but Barker who had been a magnificent player with the club in the decade leading up to the war had minimal managerial experience.

He stood no chance whatsoever and by the end of the following season what would have been unthinkable a few years earlier had come to pass. The Baseball Ground was suddenly playing host to the likes of Workington, Gateshead and Crewe in the Third Division North and in came Harry Storer, another stalwart from the halcyon days, to take over as manager.

Storer quickly halted the decline and after just missing out on promotion at the end of the 1955-56 season, his first in charge, he went a step further a year later by leading his rejuvenated team up to Division Two. After that, despite his best efforts and with little money available to strengthen his squad, supporters had to be content with what at best could only be described as consolidation.

A final position of seventh at the end of the 1958-59 season turned out to be the best that Storer could achieve in his seven seasons with the club and a year later he decided to retire after taking the club as far as he could.

Tim Ward, the ex-Derby and England international wing-half, was recruited from Barnsley to replace him but the Rams' faithful had to remain content with modest Second Division fare well into the mid-1960s. Encouragingly, there were a few promising youngsters coming through from the junior ranks including Ron Webster and Peter Daniel. Storer had also brought in Alan Durban, a fine young midfielder from Cardiff City. Unfortunately, with little or no money in the bank and a largely unambitious board of directors running the club, the most likely exit from the second tier of English football at a gloomy and dispiriting Baseball Ground was in a downwards direction rather than promotion.

Supporters had to wait until 1966 for the next signing of any real significance when Tim Ward persuaded the board to splash out on Kevin Hector, Bradford's prolific young striker. It was well worth the wait and although no one dreamt it at the time, something extremely exciting was about to unfold.

Ward's contract was not renewed and in the summer of 1967 chairman Sam Longson decided to take a gamble on an ambitious young manager from Hartlepools United called Brian Clough after being contacted by Len Shackleton, the ex-Sunderland player. If anyone could shake a moribund football club out of its lethargy he could, but it would have to be done with the help of his assistant Peter Taylor who was already building up a reputation for spotting talented young players. A year later in came the inspirational Dave Mackay from Tottenham Hotspur to captain his exciting young squad which by then included new signings Roy McFarland, John O'Hare and ex-Forest winger Alan Hinton. Midfielder Willie Carlin was recruited from Sheffield United in August 1968 and promotion was won at a canter the following April.

The eagerly awaited 1969-70 season was Derby's first in the top flight since 1953. It got underway at the Baseball Ground in early August with a goalless draw against Burnley and after going undefeated in their opening 11 fixtures the Rams led the table for the first time since 1948. Although they fell away in mid-season, a fine run of results from February onwards enabled Clough's side to finish in a highly creditable fourth place. They had exceeded the expectations of all but the most fanciful supporter and with Terry Hennessey the only major signing, they had done so with virtually the same small group of players that had won promotion a year earlier. It was a remarkable achievement.

The 1970-71 season turned out to be more difficult. After an encouraging start Derby were in fourth place at the end of August and a few weeks later Archie Gemmill was signed from Preston to replace the popular Willie Carlin. A series of injuries stretched the small squad to the limit and at one stage Derby had plummeted to an extremely worrying position of fourth from bottom. Colin Boulton replaced Les Green in goal at the turn of the year and in February Clough amazed everyone, including chairman Longson, by signing Colin Todd from Sunderland for a British record transfer fee for a defender. Results began to improve and with McFarland and Todd quickly forging an excellent partnership the Rams finished the season in ninth place.

After playing in all 42 League matches skipper Dave Mackay bid an emotional farewell following the last match of the season at home to West Brom and moved to Swindon Town as player-manager. A truly great player, he had enjoyed a glorious career stretching back 20 years with Heart of Midlothian, Tottenham Hotspur and Derby and his presence at the Baseball Ground would be missed. He had been an inspirational captain as well as remaining a fine player and with Todd already in place Clough solved the captaincy problem by handing the job to Roy McFarland.

Although the 1970-71 season as a whole had been disappointing compared to the previous one, it had ended on a surge of optimism despite Mackay's exit. So just in case anyone was expecting Derby to win the title when the players reported back for training in July 1971, Clough was already making it clear that his side had no chance whatsoever. Don Revie's formidable Leeds United were the favourites and current double holders Arsenal were bound to be in the running as would Bill Shankly's powerful Liverpool side. All had far greater resources than Derby as had Manchester United, although many observers were of the opinion that Busby's men were in decline.

There was precious little cover across Clough's squad, which consisted of 13 experienced first teamers and a handful of fringe players. Colin Boulton who was now recognised as one of the finest 'keepers around thanks mainly to his sheer consistency would be certain of his place. There was no one to challenge him for the goalie's jersey although there were persistent rumours that the manager had noted a promising young 'keeper called Peter Shilton.

Although Peter Daniel was still on Derby's books he had rarely featured since Clough replaced Tim Ward as manager, which left Ron Webster and John Robson as the only recognised full-backs although Colin Todd was capable of playing at right-back if absolutely necessary.

Roy McFarland and Todd were automatic choices in central defence and there was Terry Hennessey to fit in somehow; fitness permitting. Archie Gemmill was a certain starter in midfield but Alan Durban and John McGovern might have to vie for the other place if the manager opted for a 4-2-4 formation. Clough rated McGovern extremely highly but Durban, who was more likely to find the back of the net, couldn't be written off. If he decided that an extra man in midfield was necessary then Durban would be handed a place unless Hennessey was asked to play further forward.

A 4-3-3 line-up would almost certainly mean that once again there would be no place for Frank Wignall who, on his day, was still capable of adding extra fire power up front alongside John O'Hare, Kevin Hector and winger Alan Hinton. Fine player though Hector was, his goal tally had been slightly disappointing for a couple of years although, to be fair, Clough had often asked him to play in a slightly withdrawn position. He had looked comfortable enough there but it had restricted his opportunities in front of goal. As for O'Hare, as far as the manager was concerned, he was indispensable

Hinton was certain to fill the left wing berth. His exceptional crossing and shooting were a key component and although there was some criticism among supporters of his unwillingness to track back and tackle, the manager was shrewd enough to concentrate on his strengths rather than worry about any perceived weaknesses.

In the meantime there had been rumours that Clough had been looking for ways to increase the size and quality of his squad. There was very little cover up front and although Wignall was still an option, an injury to Hector or O'Hare would be extremely disruptive. By now the name of Jeff Astle, the West Brom and England centre-forward, was constantly cropping up. The manager was also rumoured to have been making inquiries about Hull City striker Ken Wagstaff who was highly rated by Peter Taylor.

Pre-season Preparation

When the fixtures for the 1971-72 season came out in June Derby County fans were greeted with the thrilling news that not only would the first match be at home, but that the visitors would none other than Manchester United. It was an exciting prospect but there may have been a degree of apprehension too.

Pre-season preparation was to be concluded in late July and early August by a short trip to Germany and Holland to play against Schalke 04 and Werder Bremen before taking on Dutch side Go Ahead Deventer. A few days later a return match with Shalke was planned to take place at the Baseball Ground. By the time they set off on the tour, almost a quarter of a million pounds worth of season tickets had been sold. There were tentative plans to upgrade the Baseball Ground too. The capacity at the time was just over 40,000 of which only approximately 13,000 was seated and an overall increase of around 10,000 was being mooted including around 7,000 extra seats.

Although training was reported to be going particularly well, there were concerns about Roy McFarland who had been stricken with a bad attack of influenza and a niggling leg injury. He would play no part on the tour but there were hopes that he would recover in time to get fully fit for the start of the new season.

Wednesday 28 July

Derby County v Shalke 04

The first match on the pre-season tour took place at Gelsenkirchen on 28 July with Shalke 04 the opponents. The home side came close to opening the scoring in the first minute but were denied by a fine save from Colin Boulton. Before long Derby, who were wearing what was described as their new England style kit for the first time, began to dominate. The two midfielders, McGovern and Gemmill, were playing particularly well and Hector was looking sharp.

The Rams went ahead when Hector turned in a low shot after good work from O'Hare and Wignall and shortly afterwards the striker made it 2-0 after Hinton and Wignall had combined well. Fischer pulled a goal back for Shalke only for O'Hare to confirm the Rams' superiority in the 73rd minute with a magnificent goal, flicking the ball over his shoulder and firing a fierce volley past 'keeper Nigbur. By then Durban had come on to replace Hinton and although Boulton was called on to prevent a second goal for the home side, Derby ended-up comfortable 3-1 winners.

- DERBY COUNTY: Boulton, Webster, Robson, McGovern, Hennessey, Todd, Gemmill, Wignall, O'Hare, Hector, Hinton, (sub Durban for Hinton after 64 minutes).
- RESULT: Schalke 04 1 (Fischer), Derby County 3 (Hector 2, O'Hare).

Friday 30 July

Werder Bremen v Derby County

Two days later Werder Bremen provided the opposition for Derby's second match. A couple of years earlier the same club had arrived at the Baseball Ground for a pre-season friendly which Clough's men won 6-0. It had been embarrassingly easy but no one was expecting such a one-sided contest against the German outfit this time, particularly as it was being played on their ground. The Rams began well and were 2-0 up after 17 minutes. Hinton had opened the scoring with a fine goal after collecting a rebound and firing past the 'keeper and shortly afterwards left-back Robson was on the mark from close range. Once again Gemmill and McGovern were controlling the midfield but although Derby had numerous chances they had to be content with the two-goal lead at the interval.

Werder Bremen began to get into the game after the resumption and were rewarded when Werner Weist pulled a goal back, but with Hennessey and Todd outstanding Derby never looked like conceding a second and ran out 2-1 winners.

- DERBY COUNTY: Boulton, Webster, Robson, McGovern, Hennessey, Todd, Gemmill, Wignall, O'Hare, Hector, Hinton.
- FINAL SCORE: Werder Bremen 1 (Weist), Derby County 2 (Hinton, Robson).

Tuesday 3 August

Go Ahead Deventer v Derby County

Derby's third and last match on the tour took place four days later against Dutch side Go Ahead Deventer. Clough's men began the game looking unusually apprehensive but once they got into their stride there was no stopping them. Thanks to some resolute defending from Go Ahead, the game remained scoreless at half-time, but two minutes after the resumption Hinton put his side ahead after cutting in from the left and shooting powerfully past the 'keeper. Derby continued to dominate and the alert Hector doubled the lead after 67 minutes following an excellent move.

It was encouraging to see Hennessey playing so confidently. Not only was he defending well, he was joining in the attacks too. Also making a bid for a place in the Rams' side for the opener against United was Frank Wignall who had looked particularly sharp.

- **DERBY COUNTY: Boulton, Webster, Robson, McGovern, Hennessey, Todd, Gemmill, Wignall, O'Hare, Hector, Hinton.**
- **FINAL SCORE: Go Ahead 0, Derby County 2 (Hinton, Hector).**

The tour had been extremely successful and the party returned home in a positive frame of mind after winning all three games and playing extremely well at times. Clough's starting line-up had been unchanged throughout and the only substitution was when Durban came on for Hinton in the 64th minute against Shalke. The absence of skipper McFarland through illness had been unfortunate but at least it had given Hennessey the opportunity to link up with Todd at the heart of the defence. Thankfully, the Hennessey knee had never been an issue and he had been, arguably, the best player on view.

Hector had looked sharp and there were hopes that he might be back to his best goal scoring form even if the manager opted to continue to employ him in a deeper position rather than as an out-and-out striker.

In a preview edition of *The Ram*, Derby's new newspaper-style match day programme which had been on sale for the Shalke match, it had been reported that the German press had rated the Rams as the best English side they have seen in West Germany in 10 years. 'I am really impressed with this Derby side,' wrote the Shalke manager. 'They have great players in Hennessey and Todd and lots of very good ones too like Robson and Gemmill'.

Saturday 7 August

Derby County v Shalke 04

Exactly a week before the first League game of the new season Derby were in action at the Baseball Ground in their last pre-season friendly and with McFarland still unavailable they were unchanged once again, Their opponents were Shalke 04 who they had beaten comfortably on the tour and in front of a respectable crowd for a practice match, the German side were doing everything possible early on to frustrate the Rams' attack and prevent another mauling. With up to eight men behind the ball finding a way through was soon looking particularly difficult.

Derby began to dominate the midfield; Hinton, Wignall and O'Hare were prepared to shoot given the slightest chance and even left-back Robson was surging forward, but it was Hector who opened the scoring in the 25th minute beating 'keeper Nigbur with a fine strike. Although Derby continued to look the better side it wasn't until eight minutes from time that Hinton made the game safe. O'Hare had flicked Wignall's cross towards goal but it rebounded off the 'keeper's body to the left-winger who netted easily. It was a fine way to end pre-season preparations. The squad, with the exception of McFarland, was looking in fine shape with Todd and Hennessey in particular, catching the eye.

- DERBY COUNTY: Boulton, Webster, Robson, McGovern, Hennessey, Todd, Wignall, Gemmill, O'Hare, Hector, Hinton.
- SHALKE 04: Nigbur, Sobiryay, Kremers H., Russman, Fichtel, Huhse, Lutkebohmert, Libuda, Fiscer, Holtz, Kremers E.
- FINAL SCORE: Derby County 2 (Hector, Hinton), Schalke 0.
- ATTENDANCE: 13,051.

August 1971

Up and Running

Although the month of August had begun with the final match of the pre-season tour against Go Ahead Deventer followed by the return fixture with Shalke 04 at the Baseball Ground four days later, the real business didn't start until the second Saturday of the month when the Football League season got underway.

In the days leading up to the big kick-off there had been speculation about Clough's likely line-up for the opener at home to Manchester United, particularly the question of whether skipper Roy McFarland would be able to play after his severely disrupted pre-season. A fit McFarland would be certain to take his place in the heart of the defence alongside Todd but would the manager also find a place for Hennessey who had done so well on tour? If so

Official Newspaper of Derby County F.C.

7ₚ

No. 1 (v. Manchester United, August 14, 1971)

McFarland Out, so now Hennessey is at No. 5

Skipper Roy McFarland is not fit to return to the Derby County side for the opening Division One match at home to Manchester United.

So Terry Hennessey, who will also be bidding to regain his leadership of Wales this season, retains both the No. 5 shirt and the captaincy in place of the young England centre-half.

'Roy has been troubled by the after-effects of 'flu for a fortnight. His training has suffered—he missed the Continental tour, of course—and it has been finally decided that he would not be 100% against United,' explains Manager Brian Clough.

Mr. Clough added: 'Terry's knee trouble is now a thing of the past. He has done a magnificent job so far in Roy's position, and will do so again, I am sure, in this our first League fixture.'

Team: Boulton; Webster, Robson; McGovern, Hennessey, Todd; Gemmill, Wignall, O'Hare, Hector, Hinton. Sub: Durban.

So the Rams are unchanged, fielding the side that has won four pre-season friendlies. Two interesting new names in the Central League side: Apprentice John Turner gets his first chance in goal, and Steve Powell debuts for the Club at right-half.

Terry Hennessey

WHY WE'RE HERE . . .

DERBY COUNTY are the first Football League club, and the only Football League club, to publish their own newspaper.

THE RAM is an experiment which will be closely watched by everybody throughout the football world.

From today THE RAM will be published on Friday mornings before Saturday afternoon games, and on the Wednesday mornings of midweek matches. It will be on sale at all newsagents shops, and on all news stands, throughout Derby and Derbyshire, and in the surrounding areas.

Ask your newsagent to deliver THE RAM with your morning newspapers. Derby County's official newspaper has caught on with the public in a big way. Regular orders have poured into the newsagents. SO HEAVY HAS BEEN THE DEMAND THAT MORE THAN 50,000 COPIES OF THIS ISSUE HAVE BEEN PRINTED.

You can ensure that you keep in touch with what is happening at the Baseball Ground, and throughout the football world far beyond, by ordering your copy from your newsagent.

But, remember THE RAM is not a weekly. It will be published only before every first-team home match . . . it will not

Chairman Mr. Sam Longson reads all about it!

. . .and there are 50,000 reasons

be published before away games.

Why have Derby County switched to a newspaper style? Why have we dropped the orthodox programme?

BECAUSE the orthodox programme, introduced before the turn of the century, is now outdated.

BECAUSE our fans deserve a publication which is available before the match, and available in their local shops.

BECAUSE the newspaper format offers you, our public, a better service.

BECAUSE it allows us to give you full-colour pictures of our own and visiting team stars . . . something our younger supporters have been demanding.

BECAUSE it is good sense to weld the old-style programme content with the splash techniques, and bang-up-to-date news and picture coverage, of the newspaper format.

What happens on the field, the progress of the team, is still the most important facet of football club life. We believe the present squad is perhaps the best ever to have worn the colours of Derby County F.C.

OUR AIM IS TO MAKE THE RAM WORTHY OF THE TEAM AND THE CLUB.

Judge for yourself by placing a regular order with your newsagent.

We shall be in the shops again on Wednesday morning, August 18, with news, views and pictures ready for Wednesday night's match against West Ham United (7.30).

And, remember. If you miss us in the shops you will always find a team of sellers outside and inside the ground.

You can buy THE RAM right up to the kick-off.

SOCCER CARROT TOO TASTY

ALL SET for the new season, Derby County line up for the colour camera. Left to right—Back: John Richardson (now Notts County), Jim Walker, Peter Daniel, Ken Blair, Colin Todd, Alan Durban, Ron Webster, John Robson, Terry Hennessey, John Sims, Tommy Mason. Centre: Jimmy Gordon (Trainer-Coach), Gordon Guthrie (Physiotherapist), Ricky Marlowe, Kevin Hector, John McGovern, Jeff Bourne, John O'Hare, Colin Boulton, Roy McFarland (Captain), Frank Wignall, Archie Gemmill, Alan Hinton, Tony Bailey, John Sheridan (Second-team Trainer-Coach), Mr. Brian Clough (Manager). Front: Mr. Stuart Webb (Secretary); Mr. Sydney Bradley (Director), Sir Robertson King (President), Mr. Sam Longson (Vice-President and Chairman), Mr. Fred Walters (Vice-President), Mr. 'Bill' Rudd (Director), Mr. Michael Keeling (Director), Mr. Peter Taylor (Assistant Manager). Front: Alan Lewis, Colin Griffin, Peter Phelan, John Turner, Steve Powell, David Toon, Alan Collier. Absent: Mr. 'Bob' Innes (Director), Les Green, Barry Butlin, Peter Stone, Trevor Thompson, Malcolm Rafferty.

Steve Powell signs pro —quits school

FOOTBALL with Derby County has proved to be a tastier carrot for Steve Powell than the attractions of an almost-certain University place.

The 15-year-old Derby, Derbyshire and England Schoolboys' captain has signed apprentice professional forms for The Rams. And he has quit Bemrose Grammar School.

But Derby County, delighted with their capture of the young midfield starlet whom many experts claim is another Duncan Edwards, *will see to it that he keeps up his academic studies while under their wing.*

Most of the leading First Division clubs chased Powell's signature in recent months. No wonder. The Director of Coaching for the Football Association, Allan Wade, says: 'Powell has everything.'

Steve, son of Tommy Powell, the popular County winger of the fifties, first played for England Boys when he was 14.

He went on the club's recent Continental tour 'to gain experience'. What does Powell, senior, think of his son's decision? 'It is his future. I now want him to work hard at both soccer and his studies.'

Steve promises: 'I will.'

STEVE signs, watched by proud father.

UNITED IN FULL COLOUR – PAGE SIX

then either Robson or, more likely, Webster would have to make way but that would be harsh on the reliable right-back who rarely let the side down.

Saturday 14 August

Derby County v Manchester United

Derby County supporters scanning their new newspaper-style match day programme were greeted with the news they had been half expecting. The headline on the front page read 'McFarland Out, so now Hennessey is in at No.5'. The Derby skipper was particularly disappointed not to be playing, partly because he thought he was just about fit enough to turn out but Clough refused to take a gamble after his skipper's pre-season preparation had been so badly disrupted. Although troubled by injury since arriving at the Baseball Ground two years earlier, Hennessey was a fine player so maybe McFarland's absence would not be too serious.

McGovern was selected for a place in the two-man midfield alongside Gemmill in preference to Durban who was named as 12th man. With Wignall operating up front alongside Hector and O'Hare and Hinton on the left wing, Derby's line-up looked full of goals as long as they were provided with the right service.

As for Manchester United, although they were still the biggest name in English football, Matt Busby's men had had to settle for eighth place the previous season, just ahead of the Rams, and some observers were of the opinion that they were not the force they had been a couple of years earlier. Nevertheless, they still had some great players and in their side for the opener was the formidable attacking trio of Bobby Charlton, Denis Law and George Best.

With Derby slow out of the blocks United were soon exhibiting the sort of exceptional free-flowing football with which they had become associated and fully deserved to go ahead in the 15th minute. Charlton, who was playing particularly well, started the move by whipping over an accurate free-kick to the un-marked Brian Kidd on the far post. He headed it back to Law and the Scottish international striker made no mistake from close in with a fine volley. Ten minutes later a right wing corner from Charlton evaded Best and

Hennessey before reaching Gowling who dived in to score United's second.

Although the Rams were striving hard to get into the game they were find-ing it difficult to break down the Reds' defence and 'keeper Stepney remained largely untroubled in what was turning out to be a disappointing first half for the home supporters.

United fully deserved their two-goal lead but whatever Clough said in his pep talk during the interval must have hit home. Only five minutes had elapsed when Todd passed to the onrushing Hinton. Wignall and Stepney went for his cross but the ball broke loose to Hector who placed it into the back of the unguarded net.

By now the Rams were totally in control with Wignall, in particular, giving the United defence a torrid time. Ten minutes later Best lost out to Hennessey who then passed to Hinton. His pin-point cross found O'Hare whose header rattled the crossbar before coming back to Wignall who headed home past the wrong-footed Stepney to make it 2-2.

Later Law was booked for not moving 10 yards away for a Derby free-kick and Best should have been carded for applauding referee Pugh's decision. In the end, although the Rams looked more likely to get the deciding goal, both sides had to settle for a point from an entertaining game that had been played in difficult conditions on a rainy afternoon.

- DERBY COUNTY: Boulton, Webster, Robson, McGovern, Hennessey, Todd, Gemmill, Wignall, O'Hare, Hector, Hinton.
- MANCHESTER UTD: Stepney, O'Neill, Dunne, Gowling, James, Sadler, Morgan, Kidd, Charlton, Law, Best.
- FINAL SCORE: Derby County 2 (Hector 50, Wignall 60), Manchester United 2 (Law 15, Gowling 25).
- REFEREE: D. Pugh. • ATTENDANCE: 35,386.

Wednesday 18 August

Derby County v West Ham United

With no further injury concerns following the opening day draw at home to Manchester United and with McFarland still unavailable Clough opted for the same XI for the Baseball Ground encounter with West Ham United the following Wednesday. This meant that Welsh international Terry Hennessey would continue to captain the side. Durban who had been due to play for the reserves the previous night was named as substitute and Clough, continuing with his attacking 4-2-4 formation, had Wignall leading the line. West Ham included England skipper Bobby Moore along with striker Geoff Hurst.

Opinion among supporters was still divided as to whether the result against United represented a point gained or a point lost but this time Derby began the match in fine style. There were less than two minutes on the clock when a Hinton corner from the left glanced off O'Hare's head at the near post before finishing up in the back of the net. Six minutes later O'Hare accepted a pass from Hector before crossing to Wignall who headed home past 'keeper Ferguson for Derby's second. It was the perfect start to the season for Wignall who had scored the equaliser against Manchester United on the Saturday. He had been little more than a bit-part player for a couple of seasons but was now justifying the manager's faith in him.

The Rams were playing some fine attacking football and with a little more luck Wignall might have added a third goal. Taylor headed off the line from Hector but with West Ham gradually forcing their way back into the game the home side's defence had to be at its best. Todd and Robson were playing particularly well but the Rams also had 'keeper Boulton to thank for keeping a clean sheet in the first half.

Derby began to fade after the interval to the frustration of the home supporters but even then a disappointing West Ham were unable to reduce the arrears. In the end although the game had not reached great heights, particularly in a disappointing second half, the Rams just about deserved the two points although as Clough said afterwards, 'they made hard work of it'.

- DERBY COUNTY: Boulton, Webster, Robson, McGovern, Hennessey, Todd, Gemmill, Wignall, O'Hare, Hector, Hinton.
- WEST HAM UTD: Ferguson, McDowell, Lampard, Bonds, Stephenson, Moore, Ayris, Best, Hurst, Taylor, Robson. Sub. Howe for Ayris (70).
- RESULT: Derby County 2 (O'Hare 2, Wignall 8), West Ham United 0.
- REFEREE: J. Hunting. • ATTENDANCE: 30,783. • POSITION: 6th.

Saturday 21 August

Leicester City v Derby County

Three days later Derby were making the short journey to Filbert Street and once again Clough's XI was unchanged with McFarland on the sidelines for the third time. As for Leicester who had beaten Nottingham Forest 2-1 on the Saturday, their line-up included left-back David Nish who would join the Rams a year later.

A large contingent of Derby supporters were at the ground hoping that their side could put one over on their newly promoted rivals. Sir Alf Ramsey was in the directors' box and early on Todd showed the England manager what a fine defender he was with a magnificent tackle on Alistair Brown. Boulton was being kept busy and did well to save a fierce shot from Brown before clearing a particularly dangerous corner.

With McFarland and Leicester's ex-Derby favourite Willie Carlin watching from the stands, Shilton had to be at his best to save from O'Hare and shortly afterwards Gemmill went close. It remained

SEASON 1971-2
LEAGUE DIVISION ONE
SATURDAY AUGUST 21st 1971.
KICK-OFF 3.00 P.M.
v
DERBY COUNTY
PRICE 5p
OFFICIAL PROGRAMME OF THE LEICESTER CITY FOOTBALL CLUB

scoreless at half-time although no one could complain about the entertainment in what was turning out to be a splendid game.

After the interval Shilton was soon back in action with a superb save from McGovern although it was Leicester's Glover who came closest to opening the scoring, but Webster intervened just as he was about to shoot. Eighteen minutes into the second half Derby went ahead after Webster had latched on to McGovern's pass before crossing to Hector and with Shilton advancing forward the striker lobbed the ball over his head and into the far corner.

It was a fine goal by the Rams marksman who was looking particularly sharp. Four minutes later the Leicester 'keeper was unable to get a hand to Hinton's centre and the ball ran to Hector who turned it on to O'Hare. His header was handled on the line leaving the referee with little option than to award a penalty. Cross was booked for his protestations and when things eventually settled down Hinton converted the spot-kick with a powerful shot low to the 'keeper's left. Derby continued to look the better side and ran out comfortable 2-0 winners.

- LEICESTER CITY: Shilton, Whitworth, Nish, Kellard, Sjoberg, Cross, Farrington, Brown, Fern, Sammels, Glover.
- DERBY COUNTY: Boulton, Webster, Robson, McGovern, Hennessey, Todd, Gemmill, Wignall, O'Hare, Hector, Hinton.
- RESULT: Leicester City 0, Derby County 2, (Hector 63, Hinton 68 pen).
- REFEREE: R. Challis. • ATTENDANCE: 35,460. • POSITION: 3rd.

Tuesday 24 August

Coventry City v Derby County

The following Tuesday Derby were on their travels again, this time to Coventry City's Highfield Road stadium. In the side for his first game of the season was centre-half and skipper Roy McFarland with Hennessey rested. Unfortunately it was about to be a disastrous afternoon for the skipper who had become increasingly frustrated by his enforced absence. Although both sides had created chances it was Coventry who eventually went ahead in the 40th minute when McFarland failed to control a through ball on the edge of the penalty area and when it bobbled off his outstretched boot Joicey was able to leave him stranded before placing an accurate shot past 'keeper Boulton.

Derby were well on top early in the second half and deservedly equalised eight minutes after the interval when Hinton's cross was punched straight to the foot of O'Hare by 'keeper Glazier allowing the Derby centre-forward to fire home unchallenged. It was his 50th League goal for Derby. Three minutes later Todd made a rare mistake and McFarland in trying to rescue the situation attempted to pass the ball back to Boulton. Unfortunately Joicey was in the right place to intercept but just as he was about to score the Derby 'keeper pulled him down. Referee Taylor had no option other than to award a penalty, which Hunt converted. Later McFarland tried to make up for his earlier errors with a close-range volley but the alert Glazier tipped it over the bar.

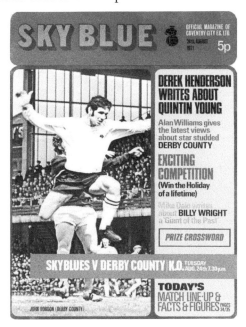

With time running out Derby eventually got a deserved equaliser when Hinton's centre was glanced home by Wignall for his third goal of the season. The draw meant that the Rams remained unbeaten after four matches – Ten altogether including the final six games of the previous season. Afterwards a disappointed Clough refused to criticise McFarland adding that as far as he was concerned, Derby deserved nothing out of the game.

- COVENTRY CITY: Glazier, Smith, Cattlin, Mortimer, Blockley, Barry, Young, Carr, Joicey, Hunt, McGuire.
- DERBY COUNTY: Boulton, Webster, Robson, McGovern, McFarland, Todd, Gemmill, Wignall, O'Hare, Hector, Hinton.
- RESULT: Coventry City 2 (Joicey 40, Hunt 57 pen), Derby County 2 (O'Hare 53, Wignall 84).
- REFEREE: J. Taylor. • ATTENDANCE: 27,752. • POSITION: 3rd.

On the front page of the newspaper-style *Ram Magazine* for the West Ham match the editor wrote that at least 45,000 copies of the previous edition had been sold. On the same page the question was asked, why is it that West Ham and England skipper Bobby Moore gets 'the bird' wherever he plays when he is the most popular player in the country?

In an article on page eight the 'knockers' who had been coming to the Baseball Ground to jeer the Rams during their friendly with Shalke and the first League match of the season against Manchester United were criticised and in other article Roy McFarland wrote, 'I will never forget my old mate Dave', referring of course to Dave Mackay who had left Derby to join Swindon Town as player-manager.

The Ram editor, David Moore (same name – no relation) reckoned that Colin Boulton had climbed into the top 10 'keepers in the country and on the following page Kevin Hector insisted he wasn't worried about not being the club's top goalscorer the previous season.

Saturday 28 August

Derby County v Southampton

Derby County were at home to Southampton the following Saturday. The Saints could be formidable opponents on their day and with some tough competitors in their squad as well as some talented ones they were likely to provide stiff opposition.

Into the Rams line-up came Durban for his first appearance of the season with Wignall making way and Hennessey was recalled after missing the Coventry match. Todd, who had been in magnificent form so far, was switched to right-back in place of Webster who had sustained an ankle injury at Coventry.

Derby were quickly off the mark and before long the visitors' defence was coming under pressure. Despite going close on a few occasions it wasn't until six minutes before the interval that they finally took the lead through McGovern. Ghosting into the penalty area the hard-working midfielder beat 'keeper Martin with a low shot which went in at the far post.

By then Southampton had switched left-back Fry to the right flank in an attempt to thwart the dangerous Hinton. O'Hare was struggling with an ankle injury and the Rams seemed to be missing the threat that Wignall had been posing in earlier matches although Martin had to be at his best on a couple of occasions to prevent further goals. The 'keeper had no chance in the 63rd minute when Hector, who was making his 200th League appearance for Derby, ran on to Hinton's high floating corner kick before breasting the ball down and firing home to make it 2-0.

Seven minutes later Southampton, who seemed to have been spurred into action by the Rams' second goal, made it an unlikely 2-1. The move started with some intricate passing in midfield and when the ball fell to Terry Paine, the lively winger fed a pass to Bobby Stokes who fired home.

Derby's defence was coming under increasing pressure and with eight minutes remaining Jenkins picked out Stokes with a fine pass. Boulton found himself out of position and Todd, doing his upmost to prevent a goal, handled the ball. He was duly booked by referee Burtenshaw before Gabriel stepped up to convert the penalty to make it 2-2. With time running out a revitalised Southampton were going flat out for the winner and the Rams' over-worked defence were relieved when referee Burtenshaw eventually blew for time.

Although Derby had dominated for long periods they were probably happy to settle for a point after the Saints' late rally although Ronnie Allen, the Athletic Bilbao coach, who was watching his side's UEFA Cup opponents, said afterwards that they should have won easily, 'I don't expect a lot of problems from Southampton', he added.

- DERBY COUNTY: Boulton, Todd, Robson, Hennessey, McFarland, McGovern, Gemmill, Durban, O'Hare, Hector, Hinton.
- SOUTHAMPTON: Martin, Kirkup, Fry, Fisher, McGrath, Gabriel, Paine, Channon, Stokes, O'Neill, Jenkins.
- RESULT: Derby County 2 (McGovern 39, Hector 63), Southampton 2 (Stokes 70, Gabriel, 82 pen).
- REFEREE: N. Burtenshaw. • ATTENDANCE: 28,498. • POSITION: 4th.

Tuesday 31 August

Ipswich Town v Derby County

Brian Clough recalled Wignall in place of the injured O'Hare for the trip to Ipswich three days later. Bobby Robson's side who were lying just below the Rams in fifth position had only conceded one goal in their first four matches and they never looked like letting the visitors add a second in a forgettable first half.

Although Derby's football was more pleasing on the eye than the home side's more direct approach, only during a short period of play in the first half when Hector began to create problems did 'keeper Best look troubled. On the rare occasions when Ipswich threatened to open the scoring the Rams' defence stood firm although Clarke twice came reasonably close. McFarland, who was being watched by Sir Alf Ramsey, was at the top of his game after his problems in pre-season and on this sort of form looked certain to retain his England place for the European Championship match against Switzerland in October.

After the interval Hector was fouled just as he was about to test the 'keeper but it was the home side which came closest to breaking the deadlock when Jefferson's powerful header went narrowly wide. Minutes later it looked as though Wignall had scored but his fine header was disallowed after an intervention by a linesman.

Although the game failed to reach any great heights, a point on the road against a side that was getting a reputation for being difficult to beat was a satisfactory outcome. Afterwards Brian Clough bemoaned Derby's lack of consistency but insisted that there were better times ahead.

OFFICIAL
PROGRAMME

6p
DERBY COUNTY
Tuesday, August 31st, 1971
Kick-off 7.30 p.m.
(DIVISION 1)

- IPSWICH TOWN: Best, Hammond, Harper, Morris, Bell, Jefferson, Robertson, Mills, Clarke, Hamilton, Miller.
- DERBY COUNTY: Boulton, Todd, Robson, Hennessey, McFarland, McGovern, Gemmill, Durban, Wignall, Hector, Hinton.
- RESULT: Ipswich Town 0, Derby County 0.
- REFEREE: K. Walker. • ATTENDANCE: 18,687. • POSITION: 3rd.

Although Derby remained unbeaten after six matches at the end of August, they had drawn four of them and had to be content with third place, four points behind leaders Sheffield United who had won five of their first six fixtures and drawn the other. Manchester United on eight points after three wins, two draws and one defeat were marginally ahead of the Rams on goal average while Liverpool who had played a game less were on the same total after four wins and one defeat.

By the end of the month McFarland, who had missed those first three games, was back in top form and it had been encouraging to see Hennessey, who had already made five appearances, making such an impact early on. Boulton had been in excellent form too and had kept clean sheets against West Ham, Leicester and Ipswich.

Gemmill had begun the new campaign full of energy as usual. The hardworking McGovern had been consistent but had still to convince his critics and Durban hadn't made an appearance until the fifth match of the season at home to Southampton. He added balance and flair to the midfield and was always likely to pop up with a goal. Hector and Wignall, with three goals each, had started the season in fine form and the splendid O'Hare was also playing well and had netted twice.

With two points for a win, the top of the First Division table at the end of August looked like this:

	P	W	D	L	F	A	Points
Sheffield United	6	5	1	0	11	2	11
Manchester U	6	3	2	1	12	7	8
Derby County	6	2	4	0	10	6	8
Liverpool	5	4	0	1	12	8	8
Stoke City	6	3	2	1	9	6	8

September 1971

Still Unbeaten

Saturday 4 September

Everton v Derby County

Brian Clough recalled full-back Webster who had recovered from injury for the trip to Everton on Saturday 4 September allowing Todd to revert to his normal position in place of Hennessey who was suffering from a thigh strain. Durban was making his 300th League appearance for Derby. The Merseysiders, who were struggling near the bottom of the table, were without centre-half Brian Labone along with mid-fielders Colin Harvey and Henry Newton, all of whom were injured. Honours were more or less even early on but in the 18th minute Howard Kendall misplaced a pass and in stole Durban to latch on to the loose ball before slipping a perfect pass to Hector. The in-form striker drew 'keeper West off his line before sliding the ball into the back of the net with the minimum of fuss. 'It was just like watching Jimmy Greaves,' remarked one observer afterwards.

Eight minutes later Kendall was forced to retire with a leg strain. On came centre-forward Joe Royle to play up front alongside Johnson but Everton were forced to re-organise even further when Jimmy Husband failed to re-appear after the interval.

With England international Alan Ball well below his best, Everton rarely troubled the Derby defence and when Wignall nipped in to take advantage of a mix-up between Darracott and West to score the second goal it was all but over. In the end the 2-0 score line was a fair reflection on what had been a comfortable win, albeit against an under strength side.

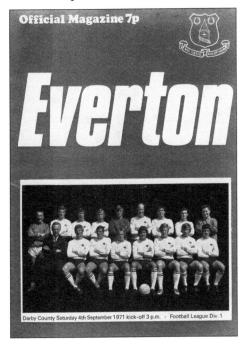

Official Magazine 7p

Everton

Derby County Saturday 4th September 1971 kick-off 3 p.m. - Football League Div. 1

After seven matches the Rams were still unbeaten and remained third behind leaders Sheffield United and second-placed Leeds. The omens were already looking good. Clough was particularly complimentary about Webster's performance on his return to the side but was concerned about the fitness of O'Hare and Hennessey, both of whom had been struggling with injuries.

- EVERTON: West, Scott, Newton K, Kendall, Kenyon, Darracott, Husband, Ball, Johnson, Hurst, Morrissey. Sub. Royle for Kendall.
- DERBY COUNTY: Boulton, Webster, Robson, Todd, McFarland, McGovern, Gemmill, Durban, Wignall, Hector, Hinton.
- RESULT: Everton 0, Derby County 2 (Hector 18, Wignall 72).
- REFEREE: A. Oliver. • ATTENDANCE: 41,024. • POSITION: 3rd.

Saturday 11 September

Derby County v Stoke City

Although Derby were still unbeaten after their first seven games, four of them had been drawn. What the second largest crowd of the season at the Baseball Ground wanted was a comprehensive victory and with Stoke in fifth place is wasn't likely to be easy. In midweek the Rams had drawn 0-0 with Leeds United in a fiercely contested League Cup tie at the Baseball Ground in a match that had seen the return of O'Hare after a two game absence.

Thankfully, he had come through unscathed and would be wearing the number nine shirt playing alongside Wignall against the Potters. With McGovern out through injury, the manager made a couple of positional changes involving Gemmill and Durban.

Dennis Smith, Stoke's hard-tackling centre-half, was booked early on but although the Rams were threatening to overrun the visitors it wasn't until the 29th minute that they eventually took the lead when a short corner from the outstanding Hinton went to Todd who unleashed a ferocious shot from the edge of the area which whistled past Gordon Banks. It was his first goal for the club. O'Hare made it 2-0 a couple of minutes later with a fine header from another Hinton flag-kick which had sailed over the strangely out-of-sorts England 'keeper.

Hinton was having a field day and three minutes into the second half Wignall allowed Hector's cross to run through to the winger who volleyed the waist-high ball into the back of the net from close range. A rampant Derby continued on the attack and with a minute of normal time remaining Gemmill was in the right place at the right time to fire home and make the final score 4-0.

Afterwards Tony Waddington, the Stoke manager, praised the Rams and in particular Colin Todd who he said, 'looks to have greatness in him.' before adding. 'he does the kind of job Bobby Moore does for England but tonight he did it better than Moore can'. Brian Clough plumped for Hinton as his man of the match. 'He was fantastic; long balls, short corners, free-kicks, tremendous shooting; he did the lot today,' said the manager. 'There is a long way to go', he added, 'but I'm a happy man'.

- DERBY COUNTY: Boulton, Webster, Robson, Todd, McFarland, Gemmill, Durban, Wignall, O'Hare, Hector, Hinton.
- STOKE CITY: Banks, Marsh, Pejic, Bernard, Smith, Lees, Mahoney, Greenhoff, Ritchie, Dobing, Haselgrave. Sub. Stevenson for Bernard at half-time.
- RESULT: Derby County 4 (Todd 29, O'Hare 31, Hinton 48, Gemmill 89), Stoke City 0.
- REFEREE: E. Wallace. • ATTENDANCE: 32,545. • POSITION: 2nd.

Saturday 18 September

Chelsea v Derby County

A week later Derby were away at Chelsea and back came McGovern with Durban making way. Although Clough had made other changes for a Texaco Cup match against Dundee United in mid-week, which his side had won 6-2, that was the only alteration from the side that had beaten Stoke so convincingly.

In soaring temperatures at Stamford Bridge the Rams were aiming to make it nine games unbeaten. They were quickly on the attack and although their superior skills were evident, the home side also looked dangerous, particularly when Derby became over-casual. Peter Bonetti had to be at his best to tip over a fierce shot from Gemmill and an O'Hare header was somehow scrambled clear.

As the half hour mark approached an opening goal for the visitors was beginning to look increasingly likely and it duly arrived in the 32nd minute. McFarland and Todd, both of whom who were in tremendous form, moved forward in tandem for a Hinton corner. Wignall helped the flag kick on to

McFarland who swivelled and fired home with a powerful, right foot drive. Derby were now playing some of their best football of the season and remained well on top up to half-time.

A pep talk from Chelsea manager Dave Sexton during the interval must have had the desired effect and the Rams were forced to defend in depth as the Blues surged forward. Todd was in particularly fine form, putting in a series of superbly timed tackles, but in the 67th minute winger Charlie Cooke raced past full-back Robson before crossing to Baldwin who turned the ball past Boulton for the equaliser.

With time running out an Osgood header glanced off the crossbar but it would have been an injustice had it gone in because although Chelsea had fought hard to salvage a point, most of the football had come from Clough's side.

- **CHELSEA: Bonetti, Boyle, Harris, Hollins, Webb, Hinton, Cooke, Baldwin, Osgood, Hudson, Houseman.**
- **DERBY COUNTY: Boulton, Webster, Robson, Todd, McFarland, McGovern, Gemmill, Wignall, O'Hare, Hector, Hinton.**
- **RESULT: Chelsea 1 (Baldwin 67), Derby County 1 (McFarland 32).**
- **REFEREE: R. Nicholson. • ATTENDANCE: 42,872. • POSITION: 3rd.**

Saturday 25 September

Derby County v West Bromwich Albion

West Bromwich Albion were Derby's opponents at the Baseball Ground on Saturday 25 September and back into Clough's line-up came Durban with McGovern dropping to the bench.

Albion, who had been in poor form, came close to taking the lead early on, albeit against the run of play, when Asa Hartford found the back of the net but referee Nippard decided that Tony Brown had strayed into an offside position. Derby continued to press and came close on several occasions but the visitors, with up to nine men behind the ball at times, were holding on. Defenders John Wile and Len Cantello were booked for some over-enthusiastic tackling but on the rare occasions that Albion managed to mount any sort of counter-attack the Rams' defence held firm.

Despite their domination Derby were unable to find the net in a frustrating first half with Hector, who hadn't scored in the League since August, way below his best. Durban had been struggling with an injury and was replaced by McGovern during the interval. The Rams continued with their attractive style of football in the second half forcing a series of corners but 'keeper Jim Cumbes, who was in inspired form, saved everything that was thrown at him.

Late on Albion came close to snatching both points and Derby had Boulton to thank for brave saves at the feet of Tony Brown and Bobby Gould. Afterwards Albion striker Jeff Astle said that all Derby needed was someone to stick the ball in the net. Obviously manager Don Howe had done his homework because despite winning 14 corners to Albion's none, the Rams had been unable to break down his disciplined defence in which Kaye and Wile had been outstanding.

Afterwards there was a general consensus that it was a point lost rather than a point gained for Derby in what Brian Clough described as, 'a dull game'.

- DERBY COUNTY: Boulton, Webster, Robson, Todd, McFarland, Gemmill, Durban, Wignall, O'Hare, Hector, Hinton. Sub. McGovern for Durban.
- WEST BROM A: Cumbes, Hughes, Wilson, Cantello, Wile, Kaye, McVitie, Brown, Gould, Hope, Hartford.
- RESULT: Derby County 0 West Bromwich Albion 0.
- REFEREE: D. Nippard. • ATTENDANCE: 30,628. • POSITION: 3rd.

Although Derby had been below their best at times they were still unbeaten in the First Division after 10 matches at the end of September. The month had started with victories away at Everton and at home to Stoke City and the point gleaned from the 1-1 draw at Chelsea was welcome enough. The only real disappointment had been the lack-lustre display at home to West Brom in the scoreless draw.

Brian Clough already had a settled side and his only changes so far had been enforced through illness or injury. Alan Durban had returned to action for the Southampton game after regaining full fitness. Although a midfielder, the Welsh international had been Derby's leading scorer throughout the 1960s and was still capable of ghosting in and scoring vital goals.

As for the brilliant Colin Todd, he had showed his versatility by filling-in at full-back when Webster had dropped out for a couple of games through injury and Hennessey had done well most of the time in his five appearances.

All the same, supporters had breathed a sigh of relief when McFarland returned after missing the first three matches. By the end of September he was back to his best form and it was no coincidence that only a single goal had been conceded in League games during the month. Not just that, McFarland was on hand to score the crucial one, which allowed Derby to return home from Stamford Bridge with a 1-1 draw. By now he was regarded by most observers as the best centre-half in the country and was a fixture in Sir Alf Ramsey's side when fully fit.

Frank Wignall had played in all but one of the early games, scoring four goals in the process. But now that Clough had reverted to a three-man midfield, which included Durban, the striker's opportunities had become limited.

In the meantime a promising young striker called Roger Davies had been signed from Worcester City for a record fee for a non-League player of £14,000 and he quickly made his mark by scoring a last minute winner on his debut for the reserve side against West Brom.

The top of the First Division table at the end of September looked like this:

	P	W	D	L	F	A	Points
Sheffield United	10	8	2	0	18	6	18
Manchester United	10	6	3	1	22	13	15
Derby County	10	4	6	0	17	7	14
Manchester City	10	5	3	2	19	8	13
Leeds United	10	5	2	3	13	9	12
Wolverhampton W	10	4	4	2	14	11	12

October 1971

A Rose between two Thorns

Saturday 2 October

Newcastle United v Derby County

McGovern and Hennessey were back in Derby's side in place of Wignall and Gemmill for the match at St James' Park. Although Newcastle were languishing sixth from bottom they were unbeaten at home. The Rams were well on top early on and although skipper Frank Clark and 'keeper Iam McFaul were doing their best to stem the tide the game was becoming a stroll for Clough's side who were getting back to their best. Playing some of their best attacking football of the season so far, they were also looking solid at the back.

All the same, Derby's lack of killer instinct in front of goal was beginning

to become a concern. They were totally dominating games but goals had become increasingly scarce and only on one occasion had they scored more than two in a League game. Nevertheless, it seemed to be only a matter of time before they would find a way through the Newcastle defence and the goal, which was looking increasingly likely duly arrived in the 61st minute. Hinton was the scorer, latching on to a loose ball on the edge of the penalty area and volleying powerfully past McFaul.

Despite creating numerous chances Derby had to settle for a narrow 1-0 victory. The two points were extremely welcome after the frustrating stalemate at home to West Brom the previous Saturday. Once again Todd had been outstanding which prompted Clough to speculate why Newcastle hadn't tried to sign him from near neighbours Sunderland when he had been available.

After 11 matches Derby remained unbeaten but Sheffield United's defeat at Old Trafford against second-placed Manchester United meant that only a couple of points separated the top three clubs.

- NEWCASTLE U: McFaul, Craig, Ellison, Gibb, Howard, Clark, Barrowclough, Tudor, Macdonald, Nattrass, Hibbitt.
- DERBY COUNTY: Boulton, Webster, Robson, Todd, McFarland, Hennessey, McGovern, Durban, O'Hare, Hector, Hinton.
- RESULT: Newcastle United 0, Derby County 1 (Hinton 61).
- REFEREE: R. Kirkpatrick. • ATTENDANCE: 32,077. • POSITION: 3rd.

Saturday 9 October

Derby County v Tottenham Hotspur

Brian Clough made one change from the side that had won at Newcastle for the Baseball Ground encounter with Tottenham Hotspur, Gemmill returning after a one match absence with Hennessey making way. Spurs' star-studded line-up included Alan Mullery and Martin Peters in midfield with Alan Gilzean and Martin Chivers up front.

The biggest crowd of the season so far was anticipating an exciting encounter between two fine sides but the first half turned out to be a disjointed affair with both teams way below their best. Derby's cause wasn't helped when full-back Webster limped off with a torn muscle in his left leg after 20 minutes and on came substitute Wignall with Todd moving to right-back.

Sir Alf Ramsey was present to check up on established internationals such as McFarland and Peters as well as the likes of Todd, Hector and Chivers and it was the dangerous Tottenham striker who put the visitors ahead in the 54th minute, nodding past Boulton after Gilzean's header had rebounded to him off the cross-bar. In contrast, Derby's equaliser shortly afterwards from Todd was a spectacular effort as he hammered an unstoppable shot past Jennings from just outside the box.

With time running out the Rams were pressing hard for the winner and with six minutes remaining McFarland headed home from Hector's cross. Tottenham looked a beaten team but with two minutes of normal time left Jimmy Pearce forced home an unlikely equaliser. Once again Derby had dropped a point after looking by far the superior side, particularly in the second half.

Afterwards most neutrals were of the opinion that Spurs' goals should have been ruled out. The first looked offside and the second seemed dubious because the ball had been knocked out of Boulton's hands but Clough and his players, as usual, refused to argue with the referee's decisions.

Striker Chivers remarked that although Derby had exerted most of the pressure his side had stuck to their task before going on to say what a great prospect the Rams had in Colin Todd. This sentiment was echoed by journal-

WHY NOT BE A SPECIAL AGENT?
—See Page Ten

the Ram

7p

Official Newspaper of Derby County F.C.

No. 8 (v. Tottenham, October 9, 1971)

NOT GUILTY!

HOW COME that Rams, unbeaten in The Football League, go to Scotland and lose 3-2 in the Texaco Cup second leg tie to Dundee United, currently holding up the rest in the Scottish First Division?

That's what the rumour-mongers wanted to know, especially when Manchester City had their £1,000 participation fee withdrawn by the International Board last week after they fielded a weak side in the same round.

ARCHIE RETURN

ARCHIE GEMMILL, substitute at Newcastle, is back in the Derby County side to play Spurs. He wears the No. 7 shirt, with John McGovern moving to left-half.

Terry Hennessey, who played possibly his best game of the season against United, has a sore throat. 'He is due to make his return to the Wales side next Wednesday,' says Manager Brian Clough, 'and we do not wish to prejudice his chances in any way.'

Team: Boulton; Webster, Robson; Todd, McFarland, McGovern; Gemmill, Durban, O'Hare, Hector, Hinton. Sub.: Wignall.

Reserves (Away to Newcastle): Moseley; Stone, Lewis; Powell, Daniel, Bailey; Bourne, Butlin, Davies, Toon, Walker. Sub.: Mason.

THERE IS A SIMPLE ANSWER. Manager Brian Clough told the local Dundee paper on the morning of the game: 'We have a load of injuries, but we have come here to win. We don't like losing at Derby.'

And he telephoned South to get Terry Hennessey, who was recovering from a bout of 'flu, to rush to catch a Supporters' Charter flight leaving East Midlands Airport in mid-afternoon on match day to boost his selection.

Medical certificates

With six first-teamers nursing injuries, he had no other choice. Medical certificates proved it. Despite all this, Rams should never have lost. Two quick goals ahead, to extend their aggregate lead to 8-2 following their easy first leg win, the Rams then allowed Dundee to get back into the game and the Scots scored three goals and a consolation home win.

'I never want to see a Derby side lose so sloppily again,' Mr. Clough warned his players meaningfully after the game. Anybody hearing that would have known that no-one at Derby likes losing anything.

As a club, we consider that if an internationally famous oil company like Texaco Ltd. consider British football worth sponsoring to the tune of more than £100,000 a year. THEN IT IS THE BOUNDEN DUTY OF EVERY SIDE WHO ACCEPT THE INVITATION TO COMPETE IN THE TEXACO CUP TO FIELD ITS BEST AVAILABLE SIDE, AND TO DO EVERYTHING IT CAN TO WIN EVERY GAME.

Clubs owe it to the sponsors, to The League, and to their supporters. No-one at the Baseball Ground considers the Texaco Cup to be anything but a first-class competition. That's why we're in it . . . AND THAT'S WHY WE HOPE TO WIN IT.

TEXACO

RAM PIN-UP
Wales star
ALAN DURBAN

Don't go North, young man...

WHAT A SHOCK for the Rams' players when they met Dundee United in Scotland last week. There has been no 'Big Clean Up' North of the Border.

Don't get us wrong. It wasn't a dirty game, and the Scottish team did nothing about which anyone would complain, but it was all so different.

The tackle from behind is still allowed, heavy challenges invoke almost no response from referees . . . in fact it was just like our football used to be until this season.

Brian Clough told Ram 'It isn't until you see a game played as we used to do that you realise just how much an advance we have made.'

League clubs coming back from European dates during the past fortnight have all reported surprise at the tremendous sweep achieved by The Football League 'Clean Up' this season.

'Nowhere are players getting the chance to work the ball as they are in England now,' they all report. On the Continent the jersey-tugging, the body-checking, the ankle-tapping, and all the sophisticated tricks, are going on apace under the eyes of benevolent referees. NOT HERE.

And if our own Rams' players are any guide to the general feeling in dressing rooms up and down the country, the verdict can only be: WELL DONE, FOOTBALL LEAGUE.

The Ram	The Ram
DERBY COUNTY	
4	
Voucher	

OFFICIAL NEWSPAPER AND PROGRAMME

ists, one of whom described him as the new Crown Prince of English soccer and head and shoulders above the rest of the internationals on show.

By now some Derby supporters were beginning to talk about their side's chances of lifting the First Division trophy but Clough was not quite so optimistic and was critical of his players' inability to hold on to a lead.

- DERBY COUNTY: Boulton, Webster, Robson, Todd, McFarland, McGovern, Gemmill, Durban, O'Hare, Hector, Hinton. Sub Wignall for Webster.
- TOTTENHAM H: Jennings, Evans, Knowles, Mullery, Collins, Beal, Pearce, Perryman, Chivers, Peters, Gilzean. Sub. Pratt for Knowles.
- RESULT: Derby County 2 (Todd 67, McFarland 84), Tottenham Hotspur 2 (Chivers 54, Pearce 88).
- REFEREE: C. Smith. • ATTENDANCE: 35,744. • POSITION: 4th.

Saturday 16 October

Manchester United v Derby County

The following Saturday Derby were off to Old Trafford to take on second placed Manchester United. With Webster unavailable because of the leg injury picked up against Spurs, Hennessey returned to the side with Todd taking over at right-back. As for United, although Law and Charlton might be past their brilliant best, they were still extremely dangerous. There were increasing concerns about George Best's off-field activities but he was still unstoppable on his day.

Early on it was becoming obvious that Derby were up against United at their very best and they were extremely lucky to go in at half-time without conceding a goal. Both Kidd and Gowling had rattled the woodwork and it was just as well for the Rams that Todd and McFarland were in top form but Boulton had to be alert on several occasions to keep a clean sheet.

United continued to surge forward after the resumption and the over-worked Derby defence was under continual pressure. It seemed only a matter of time before Busby's side broke through but when the inevitable goal arrived in the 52nd minute it was a scrappy affair, the elusive Best stabbing the ball home after the over-worked Boulton had miss-punched in a goalmouth melee. After that

Derby never looked like finding a way back and their defence had to be at its very best to prevent the home side from increasing the lead.

Derby's defeat ended an unbeaten run in the League, which had stretched to an amazing 18 games altogether including six at the end of the previous season. United's victory took them to the top of the table, three points ahead of Sheffield United with Derby fourth, one point behind on 17, the same number as Manchester City who had a better goal average.

After the match a defiant Clough said that although Manchester United deserved to win he thought his side were capable of going another 18 games without losing.

- MANCHESTER U: Stepney, O'Neill, Dunne, Gowling, James, Sadler, Morgan, Kidd, Charlton, Law, Best.
- DERBY COUNTY: Boulton, Todd, Robson, Hennessey, McFarland, McGovern, Gemmill, Durban, O'Hare, Hector, Hinton.
- RESULT: Manchester United 1 (Best 52), Derby County 0.
- REFEREE: P. Partridge. • ATTENDANCE: 53,247. • POSITION: 4th.

Saturday 23 October

Derby County v Arsenal

After their first League defeat of the season the question when double holders Arsenal arrived at the Baseball Ground the following Saturday was whether the Rams could bounce back quickly and stay in contention.

Webster was back in the side after recovering from injury allowing Todd to revert to his best position alongside McFarland in central defence with the unlucky Hennessey making way. Clough had used just 13 players in 15 League and League Cup matches so far but prior to the match he announced that he would be including 16-year-old Steve Powell in his 13-man squad. Sure enough, when the team sheets were handed in, Powell was named as substitute in preference to Wignall. As for Arsenal who had completed the double the previous season, they included the controversial Charlie George in their line-up.

In front of the biggest crowd of the season so far, Derby began the match on the front foot and before long were displaying the sort of attacking football that had made them so popular, not only with their own supporters but with television viewers across the country too. Full-back Nelson had already cleared off the line by the time the Rams went ahead in the 10th minute through O'Hare who collected a cross from Gemmill before leaving 'keeper Bob Wilson flat-footed with a fine effort.

Although the Gunners were being outplayed early on, they had refused to buckle and they got their reward in the 29th minute when Graham headed home past Boulton after getting first to a corner from the left flank. Undeterred, Derby continued to press and a minute before the interval they were awarded a penalty when the referee adjudged that Pat Rice had fouled Hector in the box. Up stepped Hinton to fire home from the spot and make it 2-1.

Although the Rams were below their best in the second half, their goal was never seriously threatened. With 20 minutes remaining debutant Powell replaced Webster and five minutes later Simpson came on for Kelly for the visitors but with further chances going begging they had to be content with a narrow victory.

After the game most pundits agreed that Derby had looked the better side overall and should have won by a bigger margin. Arsenal manager Bertie Mee praised his opponents saying that he thought they had as good a chance of winning the League title as any of their rivals, including his own side. As for Brian Clough, he considered that Derby fully deserved the victory and shrugged off questions about the controversial penalty.

- DERBY COUNTY: Boulton, Webster, Robson, Todd, McFarland, McGovern, Gemmill, Durban, O'Hare, Hector, Hinton. Sub. Powell for Webster after 70 minutes.
- ARSENAL: Wilson, Rice, Nelson, Kelly, McLintock, Roberts, Armstrong, George, Radford, Kennedy, Graham. Sub. Simpson for Kelly after 75 minutes.
- RESULT: Derby County 2 (O'Hare 10, Hinton 44 pen), Arsenal 1 (Graham 29).
- REFEREE: W. Hall. • ATTENDANCE: 36,480. • POSITION: 2nd.

Saturday 30 October

Nottingham Forest v Derby County

A strong Derby side had been involved in a friendly match at Swindon in mid-week to commemorate the opening of the club's new main stand with Wignall on the mark in the 1-1 draw but it had been good to see Dave Mackay in action for the home side.

The following Saturday the Rams made the short journey to the City Ground to take on Nottingham Forest. By now the rivalry between the two clubs and their supporters was reaching fever pitch so as far as most Derby fans were concerned this was the most important match so far. In the match day programme readers were reminded that Derby had won on the last two occasions the clubs had met in Nottingham including the 4-2 extravaganza in the previous meeting while Forest had achieved something similar at the Baseball Ground.

Steve Powell, who had come on for the injured Webster against Arsenal, was making his first start for the club in front of a capacity crowd, which included 17,000 Derby supporters. As expected the atmosphere was electric and the game was only 12 minutes old when referee Smith penalised Todd for impeding Duncan McKenzie in the box. Boulton, who afterwards said he had a theory about dealing with penalties, dived the right way to save Storey-Moore's spot kick. The 'keeper didn't enlarge on it but whatever it was it worked.

McGovern was still being singled out for criticism by some Rams' fans, much to the annoyance of Brian Clough, but once again he was in top form controlling the midfield. 'I had more space than normal', he said later, 'so I was in with a chance'. Storey-Moore went close when his fierce shot came back of an upright before an out-of-sorts Hector missed the sort of chance he would normally tuck

Football League – Division One

FOREST REVIEW

OFFICIAL MATCH DAY MAGAZINE   FIVE NEW PENCE

Nottingham Forest   **Derby County**

SATURDAY, 30th OCTOBER, 1971   Kick-off 3 p.m.

away. The game remained scoreless at half-time with the Rams way below their best.

Thirteen minutes after the restart Sammy Chapman handled a Hinton header on the goal line and the former Forest and England winger calmly placed the ball on the penalty spot before sending 'keeper Hume the wrong way to put his side ahead.

Although the game had failed to reach the heights expected, the Derby faithful were rewarded with just over 10 minutes remaining when left-back Robson surged forward from deep in his own half and with the Forest defence retreating drove a fine left footer past Hume to make it 2-0 and seal the victory.

Afterwards the Derby manager said that despite the two points he rated this as one of his side's poorest performances of the season and confessed to giving McFarland and Todd half-time rollickings.

- NOTTINGHAM F: Hulme, O'Kane, Fraser, Chapman, Hindley, Richardson, Lyons, McKenzie, Buckley, Robertson, Storey-Moore.
- DERBY COUNTY: Boulton, Webster, Robson, Powell, McFarland, Todd, McGovern, Gemmill, O'Hare, Hector, Hinton.
- RESULT: Nottingham Forest 0, Derby County 2 (Hinton, 58 pen, Robson 79).
- REFEREE: D. Smith. • ATTENDANCE: 37,170. • POSITION: 2nd.

Although October had seen Derby beaten in the League for the first time, the three wins and a draw from the other four games during the month had been enough to lift them into second place behind Manchester United and just ahead of their local rivals from Maine Road. A rose between two thorns, maybe. The home win against Arsenal had been particularly encouraging but as far as supporters were concerned the victory at the City Ground was the highlight of the season so far, even if the Rams had not been at their best on the day.

Sheffield United, who had led the table earlier in the season, had fallen away badly after losing four matches and drawing the other but in-form Manchester City and Leeds were hot on Derby's heels. Arsenal were also mounting a challenge thanks to four wins out of five with their only defeat in October being the 2-1 reversal at the Baseball Ground.

A feature of the month had been the consistency of left-back John Robson. His contribution was often taken for granted but, as usual, his defending had been of a high standard and his passing invariably neat and accurate. Also catching the eye were some surging runs down the left-wing and the highlight of October was surely Robson's unexpected goal against Nottingham Forest at the City Ground.

The top of the First Division table at the end of October was as follows:

	P	W	D	L	F	A	Points
Manchester United	15	10	3	2	29	14	23
Derby County	15	7	7	1	24	11	21
Manchester City	15	8	4	3	25	13	20
Leeds United	15	8	3	4	21	14	19
Sheffield United	15	8	3	4	24	17	19
Arsenal	14	9	0	5	22	13	18
Liverpool	15	7	4	4	21	17	18

November 1971

Those Away Day Blues

Saturday 6 November

Derby County v Crystal Palace

Second placed Derby's first match in November was a Baseball Ground encounter with bottom-of-the-table Crystal Palace. Another two points surely. The away win against Forest at the City Ground at the end of October had been rapturously received by supporters and now they were looking forward to an eminently winnable home match. Palace had been promoted as runners-up behind the Rams at the end of the 1968-69 season but since then the fortunes of the two clubs had been in stark contrast and now the London side were struggling to maintain their place in the top tier.

With McFarland out with back trouble, in came Hennessey for only his eighth start of the season in League games. Durban and Wignall were also included with Powell and the unfit Gemmill making way. The Rams went ahead as early as the third minute with a bizarre own goal. Bobby Bell was racing back towards his penalty box trying to shake off O'Hare but when he attempted to pass the ball back to goalkeeper Jackson who was positioned at the near post his misplaced effort left the 'keeper flat-footed and the ball flew into the back of the net.

Derby were soon in total control and the only surprise was that it took until the second half to increase the lead. They had missed a number of chances in the first period with Hector struggling to find his best form in front of goal. Four minutes after the interval Wignall soared to head home in fine style from a Hinton corner.

After that the Rams' defence coped comfortably and the 2-0 lead was never seriously threatened. Although the approach work was impressive their finishing was way below par and despite dominating possession it wasn't until two minutes from normal time that they added a third goal through Hector who finished an attack in fine style.

Afterwards Brian Clough said that although he was happy with the two points he thought his side had created enough chances to win half a dozen matches. Sub-standard finishing had led to more speculation that Clough was on the lookout for a striker to boost his attacking options although by then Roger Davies was scoring goals in the reserve side. Shortly after the Palace game Frank Wignall was transferred to Mansfield Town. The ex-Forest striker had proved a shrewd signing back in 1968 but now it was time to move on.

- **DERBY COUNTY: Boulton, Webster, Robson, Todd, Hennessey, McGovern, Durban, Wignall, O'Hare, Hector, Hinton.**
- **CRYSTAL PALACE: Jackson, Payne, Bell, Blyth, Wall, Goodwin, Tambling, Craven, Hughes, Wallace, Taylor.**
- **RESULT: Derby County 3 (Bell 3 og, Wignall 49, Hector 88), Crystal Palace 0.**
- **REFEREE: E. Jolly. • ATTENDANCE: 30,388. • POSITION: 2nd.**

Saturday 13 November

Wolverhampton Wanderers v Derby County

The following Saturday Derby were away at Molyneux against a Wolverhampton Wanderers side who were struggling seventh from bottom. Surprisingly, considering the size of the squad and other commitments such as the Texaco Cup, the Rams had opted to play a friendly match against Werder Bremen on the Monday evening only two days after the 3-0 win against Crystal Palace. Even more unexpected had been the decision by the manager to field virtually a full strength side although McFarland and Gemmill had been given the night off. Derby completely overwhelmed the German Bundesliga outfit, winning a one-sided encounter 6-2 in front of over 6,000 fans.

McFarland and Gemmill returned to the line-up for the Wolves match replacing Durban and the departed Wignall and Wolves included the colourful Derek Dougan at centre-forward. Both sides had chances early on but halfway through the first period a Hinton free-kick was only partially cleared by McAlle and the ball fell to the alert O'Hare who nodded home past 'keeper Parkes to put the Rams ahead,

McFarland came close to increasing the lead with an excellent header from a Webster cross but the ball skidded narrowly wide after taking a bad bounce. Afterwards Hector said he might have got a foot to it but the ball had run away from him at the last moment.

Derby were looking comfortable but with only a minute to go before half-time they were pegged back with a soft goal from Richards. For once, the normally reliable Boulton had to take a share of the blame after he failed to get a hand to a free-kick

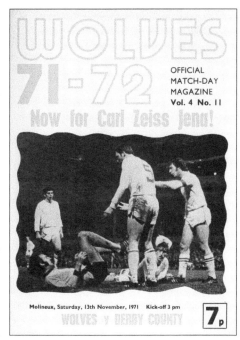

WOLVES

71-72

OFFICIAL
MATCH-DAY
MAGAZINE
Vol. 4 No. 11

Now for Carl Zeiss Jena!

Molineux, Saturday, 13th November, 1971   Kick-off 3 pm

WOLVES v DERBY COUNTY

7p

and the ball fell to the young striker who scored with relative ease. Although the Rams had looked the better side they had failed to take advantage of some sloppy Wolves defending and had paid the price.

Dougan was proving a real handful for the normally assured McFarland who was finding it difficult to cope with his aerial threat and winger Wagstaffe was giving full-back Webster a torrid time too. The Rams were battling hard to regain the lead but to the huge disappointment of the large contingent from the East Midlands the crucial third goal of the afternoon in the 78th minute went to the home side. Boulton had done well to get to a powerful strike from Kenny Hibbitt but he was unable to hold on to the ball and it fell to Dougan whose shot eventually rebounded to Richards and he applied the finishing touch to make it 2-1. Try as they could, Clough's men were unable to force an equaliser.

Afterwards one reporter described the match as an old fashioned, honest-to-goodness scrap between two talented and determined sides. Clough said he was getting used to teams raising their game against Derby. All the same, it was a set back, which had seen them fall three points behind Manchester United at the top and although they remained second, they were now on the same number of points as Manchester City and Sheffield United.

- WOLVERHAMPTON W: Parkes, Shaw, Parkin, Bailey, Munro, McAlle, McCalliog, Hibbitt, Dougan, Richards, Wagstaffe.
- DERBY COUNTY: Boulton, Webster, Robson, Todd, McFarland, Hennessey, McGovern, Gemmill, O'Hare, Hector, Hinton.
- RESULT: Wolverhampton Wanderers 2 (Richards 44, 78), Derby County 1 (O'Hare 23).
- REFEREE: D. Laing. • ATTENDANCE: 32,326. • POSITION: 2nd.

Saturday 20 November

Derby County v Sheffield United

Derby's opponents at the Baseball Ground a week later were Sheffield United. The Blades had led the table until early October before slipping down to fourth after a dip in form. Clough wrote in *The Ram* about the increase in 'physical stuff' his side had been subjected to in their last two games and hoped that the referee's clamp-down on over-physical football wasn't breaking down.

The manager opted for the same XI that had lost at Molyneux and on a bitterly cold Saturday afternoon was rewarded when his side went ahead in the second minute through Hector who netted his sixth of the season after United's Flynn had deflected a pass from Hennessey into his path. After a relatively barren spell it was beginning to look as though the striker who had also scored against Palace earlier in the month was getting back to his best.

Flynn was also at fault for Derby's second goal in the 14th minute when he handled O'Hare's header on the goal line. It was a cast-iron penalty and Hinton thumped the ball past 'keeper Hope with the minimum of fuss. The Rams were playing some fine attacking football but the visitors rarely threatened thanks largely to McFarland and Hennessey who were in total control down the middle.

The 2-0 lead at the interval was the least Derby deserved but whatever United manager John Harris said at half-time must have had the desired effect and a revitalised United began to press immediately after the restart. Winger Woodward fired narrowly wide and shortly afterwards Salmons shot over. Boulton did well to keep out efforts by Hemsley and Hockey but the lively Woodward was beginning to give Robson plenty to worry about.

Derby began to re-assert their superiority and went further ahead after 64 minutes and again the goal came from the penalty spot. Hemsley maintained that the ball had struck his body but the referee was insistent that the defender had handled and this time Hinton placed the spot-kick to the 'keeper's other side to make it 3-0. Later the Blades began to lose their composure and three players, Badger, Flynn and Hockey, were all booked in less than 10 minutes. They had had no answer to McGovern and Gemmill who had dominated the midfield.

Afterwards, somewhat bizarrely, manager Harris maintained that his side had been unlucky, adding that he thought they could easily have gone 4-2 ahead and that the second penalty was harsh. One observer wrote that Derby had reduced the Yorkshire side to a bunch of ill-tempered squabblers.

Perhaps the only disappointing feature of the afternoon was the attendance of 35,326 which included around 4,000 from South Yorkshire although the rain and sleet may have put off some of the less hardy spectators. Afterwards Clough, who was becoming increasingly unhappy about attendances at the Baseball Ground, said he had no sympathy for United who got what they deserved.

Leaders Manchester United and third placed Manchester City both won on the same afternoon, as did fourth placed Leeds so Derby's victory was particularly important if they were to stay in touch with their main rivals.

- DERBY COUNTY: Boulton, Webster, Robson, Todd, McFarland, Hennessey, McGovern, Gemmill, O'Hare, Hector, Hinton.
- SHEFFIELD U: Hope, Badger, Hemsley, Flynn, Colquhoun, Hockey, Woodward, Salmons, Reece, Currie, Scullion.
- RESULT: Derby County 3 (Hector 2, Hinton 14 pen, 64 pen), Sheffield United 0.
- REFEREE: V. Batty. • ATTENDANCE: 33,326. • POSITION: 2nd.

Saturday 27 November

Huddersfield Town v Derby County

Derby County now had the opportunity to build on their victory against Sheffield United by inflicting defeat on another Yorkshire side, Huddersfield Town. Although it was an away fixture, surely there would be little doubt that if the Rams played their normal game they would be too strong for the Terriers who were struggling fifth from bottom.

The Rams were still unbeaten at the Baseball Ground but they lost two out of the previous three away from home and if they were to maintain their challenge for the title they would have to do much better on their travels.

As expected Derby started the match on the front foot and before long were totally outplaying the home side. Unfortunately, and not for the first time, they were failing to convert chances into goals. Huddersfield were lucky to be on level turns at the break after losing possession cheaply on numerous occasions although they had also showed plenty of grit and determination.

Although O'Hare was giving the home side's defence plenty to think about, he had been unable to find the back of the net in what had been a one-sided

HUDDERSFIELD TOWN AFC

official programme

5p

SEASON 1971-72

FIRST DIVISION FOOTBALL

DERBY COUNTY

Saturday, November 27th, 1971   Kick-off 3.00 p.m.

first half but he did come close on one occasion with a header which came back off the post.

The Terriers continued to live up to their nickname by scrapping away in the second half and got their reward in the 63rd minute when the enigmatic Frank Worthington beat 'keeper Boulton for the opening goal. Although Clough's men responded with a flurry of attacks it was the home side which snatched the crucial second goal 12 minutes later through Jimmy Lawson, much to the dismay of the travelling supporters.

Derby pulled a goal back a minute later through McGovern after being put through by Hector but they were unable to add a second despite continual pressure and the match ended in an unexpected 2-1 defeat. It had been a frustrating afternoon because although they had outplayed the opposition for long periods, a lack of firepower up front had proved decisive.

Clough couldn't understand how his side had contrived to lose the match. Others thought that now that Wignall had moved on it was time to dip into the transfer market to provide more options in attack. Or was the manager banking on a recall for Alan Durban to do the trick?

- HUDDERSFIELD T: Lawson D, Clarke, Hutt, Jones, Ellam, Cherry, Mahoney, Smith S, Worthington, Lawson J, Chapman.
- DERBY COUNTY: Boulton, Webster, Robson, Todd, McFarland, Hennessey, McGovern, Gemmill, O'Hare, Hector, Hinton.
- RESULT: Huddersfield Town 2 (Worthington 63, Lawson J 75), Derby County 1 (McGovern 76).
- REFEREE: G. Hill. • ATTENDANCE: 15,329. • POSITION: 3rd.

Top of the table at the end of November were Manchester United, three points ahead of their near neighbours. Third placed Derby were on 25 points, the same number as Sheffield United and Leeds.

Manchester United's month had started with a local derby at Old Trafford which had ended in a 3-3 draw but following that match both sides had gone on to win their remaining three fixtures. Derby's two victories and a couple of draws had seen them drop one place and although Sheffield United had been well beaten by Derby they came back strongly the following weekend with a 7-0 thumping of Ipswich Town. Liverpool had maintained their challenge by winning three out of four but Arsenal had a thoroughly miserable November and were overtaken by their arch-rivals Spurs.

Alan Hinton was probably at his peak during the 1971-72 season and would eventually finish as the club's leading scorer ahead of O'Hare and Hector. Although there had been fewer than usual of his spectacular long-range goals, his total of six by the end of November, which included no less than four penalties was a fair return.

But it wasn't just Hinton's goals that were marking him out as arguably the most dangerous winger in the country; his accurate corners and crosses from open play and free-kicks were proving invaluable. November had been another productive month for him with a brace of penalties against Sheffield United and assists from corners and free-kicks in other matches.

During the month Wignall had been transferred to Third Division Mansfield with his job done. Therefore the size of the first team squad had been reduced from effectively 13 to 12. Surely either new blood would be brought in or a couple of players would need to step up from the reserves.

Top of the First Division at the end of November was as follows:

	P	W	D	L	F	A	Points
Manchester United	19	13	4	2	43	22	30
Manchester City	19	11	5	3	36	17	27
Derby County	19	9	7	3	32	15	25
Sheffield United	19	11	3	5	35	21	25
Leeds United	19	11	3	5	27	17	25
Liverpool	19	10	4	5	27	20	24
Tottenham H	19	8	6	5	36	25	22

December 1971

Halfway to Paradise

Saturday 4 December

Derby County v Manchester City

Although Derby's away form was becoming a cause for concern following successive defeats at Wolves and Huddersfield they were still unbeaten at the Baseball Ground when high flying Manchester City came to town on the first Saturday in December.

After 19 League games manager Brian Clough had used just 14 players including the departed Frank Wignall and five of them, Boulton, Webster, Todd, Hector and Hinton had played in every one. His line-up for the match against City showed one change from the side that had let themselves down at lowly Huddersfield with Durban returning and Hennessey making way. Maybe he could add some extra goal threat. Malcolm Allison, City's charismatic manager, was able to field his strongest side, which included Mike Summerbee, Colin Bell and Francis Lee.

The atmosphere was tense at a packed Baseball Ground and before long the game was living up to expectations. The Rams were looking lively and fully deserved to go ahead in the 23rd minute after McGovern was tripped in the box. A confident Hinton placed the ball on the spot before sending 'keeper Joe Corrigan the wrong way for his fifth penalty of the season and his fiftieth goal for the club.

Derby had already scored some outstanding goals in earlier matches but a rare header by full-back Webster was about to become a contender for goal of the season. Hinton, who had been giving full-back Tony Book a torrid time, collected a superb pass from Durban, raced down the left-wing before crossing to the far corner of the penalty area and in came Webster who had raced 50 yards to head past the stranded Corrigan from all of 20 yards. It was only his sixth goal in around 350 games for the club but afterwards the modest defender was content to praise Hinton for his excellent cross although he did concede that his header 'wasn't bad'.

Two minutes later the Rams made it 3-0 when the rampant Hinton launched yet another accurate cross and this time it was the recalled Durban who headed home. Derby had dominated throughout most of the first half and they continued to look the better side after the re-start. Lee pulled a goal back against the run of play from the penalty spot in the 66th minute but with the Rams defence looking strong and composed a City fight-back was looking increasingly unlikely and the match ended in a well-deserved 3-1 victory.

The Rams had now leap-frogged City into second place, albeit on goal average, but were still five points behind leaders Manchester United who beat Forest 3-2 the same afternoon.

Afterwards Malcolm Allison paid tribute to Alan Hinton saying that he was a marvellous player. 'All credit to Brian Clough for being able to get him to play like this when other managers failed to make the most of his tremendous ability', Clough thought it had been a very physical match which had turned ugly at times, adding that, 'this is not the way we normally play'.

- DERBY COUNTY: Boulton, Webster, Robson, Todd, McFarland, McGovern, Durban, Gemmill, O'Hare, Hector, Hinton.
- MANCHESTER C: Corrigan, Book, Donachie, Doyle, Booth, Oakes, Summerbee, Bell, Davies, Lee, Mellor.
- RESULT: Derby County 3 (Hinton 23 pen, Webster 36, Durban 38), Manchester City 1, (Lee 66 pen).
- REFEREE: W. Johnson. • ATTENDANCE: 35,384. • POSITION: 2nd.

Saturday 11 December

Liverpool v Derby County

Derby's next opponents in the First Division were sixth-placed Liverpool. Although the Merseysiders had been struggling away from home they had a formidable record at Anfield where they had remained unbeaten for a staggering 33 matches so no one was in any doubt that it would be a stern test for the visitors.

With Robson out injured Clough decided to switch Webster to left-back and move Todd to right-back with Hennessey returning to League action after missing the Manchester City game. The star-studded Liverpool side included 'keeper Ray Clemence, hard-man Tommy Smith, Emlyn Hughes and the up-and-coming Kevin Keegan.

Derby's defence had been outstanding for most of the season but for once they were looking below par. Hennessey who had had deputised for McFarland back in August but then played only spasmodically through September and October had recently been given a run in the side and had impressed with some fine performances. Sadly, this wasn't to be his day. He was partly at fault in the 14th minute when hesitancy between himself and 'keeper Boulton allowed striker Jack Whitham to nip in and open the scoring. Whitham, who had been standing in for the injured John Toshack, was perhaps the least well-known player in the Liverpool side but he was about to have a day he would long remember.

O'Hare equalised for Derby in the 42nd minute following a Hinton corner from the left but with half-time only seconds away and the visitors at their most vulnerable immediately after scoring, Liverpool regained the lead when Whitham shrugged off a challenge from Hennessey before firing home. It was a particularly poor goal to concede and at the worst possible time.

Four minutes after the re-start O'Hare equalised for the second time from another Hinton corner only for Whitham to ghost in to complete a fine hat-trick with a tap-in after Heighway's centre had found McFarland, Todd and Hennessey all out of position.

Todd had to retire to the dressing room with a badly-broken nose on the hour mark and on came substitute Walker with McGovern, who was having an outstanding game in mid-field, moving to full-back to replace Todd. By now other Derby players were looking less than 100 per cent fit, which perhaps wasn't surprising after the gruelling schedule of matches.

Later, only the splendid McFarland prevented further goals as the home side took control. The Rams had played some decent football early on but they had faded badly after the departure of Todd.

Afterwards Bill Shankly complimented Derby saying, 'They never stopped playing football'. In fact the Reds themselves were now looking as though they could mount a serious challenge for the title. Of course, as it turned out, all would be resolved in the return fixture between the two sides at the Baseball Ground the following May.

- LIVERPOOL: Clemence, Lawler, Lindsay, Smith, Ross, Hughes, Keegan, Hall, Heighway, Whitham, Callaghan.
- DERBY COUNTY: Boulton, Todd, Webster, Hennessey, McFarland, McGovern, Durban, Gemmill, O'Hare, Hector, Hinton. Sub. Walker for Todd.
- RESULT: Liverpool 3 (Whitham 14, 44, 63), Derby County 2 (O'Hare 42, 49).
- REFEREE: C. Howell. • ATTENDANCE: 44,601. • POSITION: 4th.

Saturday 18 December

Derby County v Everton

Although the Rams were still struggling away from home their performances and, more importantly, their results at the Baseball Ground were just about enough to keep them challenging near the top. Everton were the visitors on the afternoon of Saturday 18 December and back into Clough's line-up came left back Robson after a one match absence with Webster reverting to his normal position at right-back. McGovern was handed the number six shirt in the absence of Todd who was still recovering from his broken nose. Everton's side included Henry Newton, rumoured to be coveted by Clough, and also in their side were England internationals Alan Ball and Joe Royle.

After the defeat at Anfield Clough had taken his players to Greece for a few days to re-charge their batteries but they also played a light-hearted friendly against Olympiakos, which they lost 3-1.

With Christmas just around the corner the lure of some festive shopping must have deterred some regulars from getting to the match because the Baseball Ground didn't look as full as normal. Afterwards the attendance was confirmed at just under 28,000 which was the lowest of the season so far.

Derby were by far the better side early on with O'Hare and McGovern prominent. O'Hare's close control was exceptional and McGovern was totally outshining Ball who might have had other things on his mind with a transfer to Arsenal on the cards.

In fact the whole Everton side were looking jaded and 'keeper Boulton was enjoying one of his easiest afternoons of the season. How it remained scoreless at half time was a mystery, particularly as Hinton was also in top form, putting over a series of pin-point crosses as well as testing 'keeper Gordon West with some typically powerful shooting.

The Rams had the winger to thank when they eventually opened the scoring shortly after the interval although West might have done better to cope with his free-kick from distance which finished up in the back of the net. But the 'keeper had no chance at all in the 56th minute when Hinton let fly with another powerful shot that left him clutching at fresh air.

the Ram 7p

Official Newspaper of Derby County F.C.

No. 16 (v. Everton, December 18, 1971)

AFTER FOUR AWAY DEFEATS

TRAVEL SICK?

Derby County chairman, Mr. Sam Longson, sends this message to all supporters: 'On behalf of the President, Board of Directors, Manager, players and staff of Derby County FC, I send all our supporters and well wishers our sincere good wishes for a Happy Christmas, and a Prosperous New Year, in which we may all see even more exciting and progressive football from the team.'

FOUR DEFEATS in consecutive matches have sparked off a controversy: ARE DERBY COUNTY GOOD ENOUGH ON THEIR TRAVELS?

Defeats at Manchester United, Wolves, Huddersfield and at Liverpool last Saturday, have disrupted the impetus of the fierce Championship challenge which has been maintained right from the start of the season.

Manager Brian Clough is typically frank about the cause: 'WE LOST THESE GAMES SIMPLY BECAUSE WE WEREN'T GOOD ENOUGH ON THE DAY. We went to Anfield with the best defence in The League, having conceded only eight goals in ten games away . . . and promptly gave away three gifts. That's got nothing to do with form, that's rank bad play.'

It's a handicap

Mr. Clough underlines his previous warnings to the over-exuberant who, a few weeks ago saw The League Championship trophy already on a Baseball Ground sideboard. 'I HAVE POINTED OUT SEVERAL TIMES THAT THE LACK OF STRENGTH IN DEPTH OF THE FIRST-TEAM SQUAD AT THIS STAGE OF OUR DEVELOPMENT INTO A TOP CLASS CLUB COULD WELL BECOME A REAL DIFFICULTY.

Last Saturday's injury to Colin Todd underpins Mr. Clough's problem. The badly broken nose was the result of an accidental elbow from Liverpool winger Kevin Keegan, and the plaster which envelops Colin's nose and forehead can't come off for a fortnight. IN ADDITION TO MISSING THE EVERTON MATCH IT IS ALMOST CERTAIN TODD WILL ALSO MISS THE VITAL BOXING DAY MATCH AT LEEDS.

The manager insists he has lost one-sixth of his squad's strength in one fell swoop. 'That is what I mean when I voice caution,' he told us. 'We do not have the squad strength to compare with Manchester United or City, Liverpool or Leeds. Leeds, for example, have been playing an England full back, Reaney, as a substitute because the current England full back Paul Madeley has taken his place.

'We just do not have that situation yet.

IS THE DERBY COUNTY MANAGER DESPONDENT, THEN? NOT ON YOUR LIFE.

'We will maintain our challenge for a top place,' he prognosticates firmly. 'We have problems with a small first team squad which we will eradicate as the club develops, BUT WE HAVE A STAR QUALITY SQUAD WITH STAR QUALITY SPIRIT.'

And he produces an example to illustrate his point: 'When Colin Todd was being rushed to hospital after he had had to come off the field in a hurry at Liverpool last Saturday, his face was stained with blood from his nose which also enveloped the towel he had wrapped round him. BUT HE STILL TURNED ROUND TO OUR PHYSIO GORDON GUTHRIE WHO ACCOMPANIED HIM, DESPITE INTENSE PAIN, AND ASKED 'DID THE BOSS SAY ABOUT THAT THIRD GOAL?'

'WITH A SPIRIT LIKE THAT GOING FOR YOU, THE TEAM MUST BE IN WITH A GREAT CHANCE.'

Brian Clough as a cricket chief?

COULD BRIAN CLOUGH perform for Yorkshire County Cricket Club a similar kind of rescue operation that he has stage-managed so brilliantly for Derby County?

The question is a pertinent one, bearing in mind his love of the Summer game in general, his close friendship with Yorkshire captain Geoff Boycott.

'There's no doubt in my mind,' says the 31-year-old Boycott, 'that county cricket teams would benefit from the appointment of a team manager.

'This applies particularly to the captain, who has to combine some of the jobs Brian does for Derby.

'It can all be terribly wearing on this one individual, and I am sure that cricket has a great deal to learn from soccer in this respect.

'BRIAN AND I MEET QUITE OFTEN. HE COMES TO WATCH ME DURING THE SUMMER, AND I AM ENJOYING WATCHING HIS TEAM PLAY THIS WINTER.'

Over to Brian Clough, who, as a staunch Yorkshireman, admits to being disappointed at the general level of results achieved by the county during recent years.

'The talent is still there in Yorkshire, but I am convinced that they need to rethink their basic approach.'

Boycott, who has maintained his own tremendously high level of performance with the bat despite the problems of captaincy, backs that up.

'Some people say I take coaching and net practice to extreme lengths. This may seem so to them because of the contrast with the majority of cricketers, who do not wish to practice.

'I feel that I am only displaying the kind of professionalism that is necessary to success in all sports. We in cricket have so much to learn from others in this respect.

'A team manager is a top priority. Touring parties have one, and this is why I enjoy playing abroad much more than in this country. But things change so slowly in county cricket . . . it could take years.'

Rams say 'No' to South Americans

DERBY COUNTY this week turned down the opportunity of gaining further international experience in a game against Nationale Montivido of Uruguay, who are contesting the World Club Championship with Panathinaikos of Greece.

The South Americans who drew 1-1 with the Greeks in Athens on Wednesday in the first leg of the world title decider, wanted to stay on and play a friendly against the Rams today (Friday).

'But we had to say no because of our commitments at home,' said Assistant Manager, Peter Taylor, who took a party of 13 players (including Peter Daniel and Jeff Bourne) to Athens last Sunday for four days' break and a match against Olympiakos Piraeus—managed by Alan Ashman—in Athens on the Tuesday.

The Rams, fielding for the full 90 minutes the side that will do duty against Everton in the League, with John Robson back in action, were beaten 3-1.

'We could have got two or three more goals,' added Mr. Taylor. 'But the main thing was that, under strict instructions, our players never retaliated despite some blatant obstruction by Olympiakos. We now have a better idea of how far we can go next time we play in Europe.' Team: Boulton; Webster, Robson; Hennessey, McFarland, McGovern; Durban, Gemmill, O'Hare, Hector, Hinton. Substitute to be named.

TEXACO FINAL

The first leg of the Texaco Cup Final between Scottish League Airdrie and Derby County will be played at Airdrie on Wednesday, January 26. The second leg is scheduled for the Baseball Ground on Wednesday, March 8.

SEARCH FOR FAN NUMBER 500,000

ONE SPECIAL DERBY COUNTY SUPPORTER IS GOING TO SPEND AN EXTRA SPECIAL SATURDAY AFTERNOON AT THE BASEBALL GROUND THIS WEEK-END.

The match against Everton will mark the five hundredth thousandth spectator paying to go through the turnstiles. And someone, somewhere, will be the man, woman or child to mark up that magic half-million figure.

Through a back-stage operation, specially mounted by Rams secretary Mr. Stuart Webb, the gate totaliser will be watched from the moment the gates open until they pinpoint the exact time and turnstile when and where Number Half Million comes through.

He or she will be noted and tagged so that they can be called on.

And that moment will come at half-time during the Everton game when Derby County chairman, Mr. S. Longson, and Mr. Webb, go out on to the pitch to invite the lucky spectator to join the Chairman and his Board in the front of the Director's box for the second half.

They will also be invited to go back-stage at the end to partake of Rams' hospitality and to accept gifts the identity of which must remain secret until

the Big Moment.

The Baseball Ground has been especially decorated with Seasonal Greetings and messages, and festooned with fairy lights which will be switched on during the afternoon.

A colourful Saturday afternoon, indeed . . .

Cup Comment

Manager Brian Clough's comment to The Ram on Derby's Third Round FA Cup draw against Third Division Shrewsbury Town at the Baseball Ground on January 15: 'It's the kind of draw to make a First Division side, with ambition to win the Cup, happy. We are happy.'

Geoff Boycott meets his pal

OFFICIAL NEWSPAPER AND PROGRAMME

McGovern with his non-stop running not only continued to keep the sub-dued Alan Ball little more than a passenger but he also found time to prompt a series of Derby attacks. In the meantime the splendid Rams' defence, ably marshalled by McFarland, remained relatively untroubled by the Everton strike force. Despite going close late on Derby had to settle for the 2-0 victory.

Afterwards O'Hare, who had given Kenyon a torrid afternoon, was being compared with Alfredo di Stefano the Real Madrid legend. Clough said that his centre-forward's performance was probably his best in a Derby County shirt. As for Hinton, it was seven years since his last international appearance and some pundits were wondering why Sir Alf Ramsey had been ignoring his claims for a recall. His powerful shooting and accurate crosses were just what England needed and as Clough said, 'Alan's second goal was something special'.

The victory saw the Rams move up into third place behind the two Manchester clubs. But if they were going to stay in contention they would have to sort out their away form. Nine days later they would be travelling to Elland Road to take on Don Revie's Leeds United and already it didn't look as though Todd would be fit enough to play. Both sides had 29 points so a particularly severe battle was anticipated.

- DERBY COUNTY: Boulton, Webster, Robson, Hennessey, McFarland, McGovern, Durban Gemmill, O'Hare, Hector, Hinton.
- EVERTON: West, Wright, McLoughlin, Kendall, Kenyon, Newton, Husband, Ball, Royle, Hurst, Whittle.
- RESULT: Derby County 2 (Hinton 49, 56), Everton 0.
- REFEREE: B. Daniels. • ATTENDANCE: 27,895. • POSITION: 3rd.

Monday 27 December

Leeds United v Derby County

Derby County were still in the running for the title but their results away from home were going from bad to worse. The two-word headline in *The Ram* for the Everton match in mid-December had posed the two-word question that was occupying the minds of many of their supporters. 'Travel Sick?'

Derby's last away win in the First Division had been at Forest's City Ground at the end of October and since then they had lost three in a row in the League, first at Wolves, then at lowly Huddersfield and finally at Liverpool. The only consolation was that all of them had been by a single goal.

If they were going to get back on track they would have to pass arguably the biggest test of all because Clough's men were about to take on Leeds United at Elland Road. Both sides were on 29 points but third placed Derby had the edge on their fierce rivals thanks to a better goal average. Worryingly, Todd was still out of contention because of his broken nose and the manager sprang a major surprise by informing young Tony Bailey an hour before the kick-off that he would be making his League debut.

The young ex-Burton Albion defender had been playing consistently well for the reserves and had turned out in three Texaco Cup matches. Although he had done well, it was totally different to playing in a crucial First Division fixture against a full-strength Leeds side.

The match started in the worst possible way for Derby. Leeds had been surging forward straight from the kick-off and were already well on top when left winger Eddie Gray swapped passes with Billy Bremner and Eddie Gray before sweeping home past 'keeper Boulton to put his side ahead in the sixth minute. By then Bailey, anxious to make his mark, had already been booked for fouling centre-forward Mick Jones.

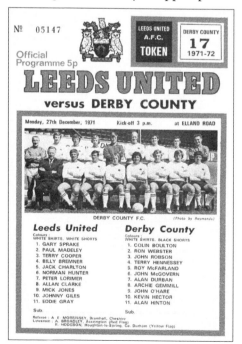

The Rams were being outplayed and it came as no surprise when the outstanding Lorimer doubled their lead 15 minutes later. Leeds continued to put the visitors' defence under constant pressure and even a fully fit Todd would probably have found it difficult to contain the powerful Elland Road front men.

It remained 2-0 at the interval

but shortly after the restart Lorimer scored his second of the afternoon, firing in from distance past Boulton. Derby's attack had never really threatened although late on they might have grabbed a consolation goal with a little more luck. It was the third match in a row that they had conceded three goals away from home but this was their heaviest defeat of the season. Surely it was time for the manager to strengthen his squad. As for Leeds, they were still a formidable outfit and had to be regarded as serious challengers for the title.

Afterwards Clough posed the question as to whether or not Derby County were tough enough, physically and mentally. 'Leeds have played us off the park and we are being outfought,' said the manager, adding that he thought that some of the players had been afraid when they ran out on to the Elland Road pitch. 'There was no shortage of skill', he said, 'but are they prepared to "dish it out", particularly away from home?'

- LEEDS UNITED: Sprake, Madeley, Cooper, Bremner, Charlton, Hunter, Lorimer, Clarke, Jones, Giles, Gray.
- DERBY COUNTY: Boulton, Webster, Robson, Bailey, McFarland, Hennessey, McGovern, Gemmill, O'Hare, Hector, Hinton.
- RESULT: Leeds United 3 (Gray 6, Lorimer 21, 58), Derby County 0.
- REFEREE: A. Morrissey. • ATTENDANCE: 44,214. • POSITION: 5th.

Derby's poor away form culminating in the extremely disappointing 3-0 defeat at Elland Road had seen them slip down the League table to fifth place. Although Manchester United had had a fairly ordinary month themselves with one win and three draws they were still top of the table, three points ahead of local rivals City.

Leeds were now very much in contention following their two wins and two draws. Sheffield United, despite losing 5-1 in early December, had bounced back with a couple of wins and a draw and although Liverpool could only manage a single victory, the one at home to the Rams, they were still handily placed in sixth. The main question now was whether the ageing Manchester United side could maintain their excellent form. If so, they would probably win the title.

The 1971-72 season was 28-year-old Ron Webster's 12th with Derby County and although they suffered those defeats at Liverpool and Leeds, conceding three goals on each occasion, little blame could be attributed to Webster who had been a model of consistency. He had also scored one of his rare goals for the club during the month, that superb header from a Hinton cross in the 3-1 victory against Manchester City, which was a reminder to some that he had begun his career with the Rams as a right sided midfielder all those years ago. The top of the First Division at the end of December looked like this:

	P	W	D	L	F	A	Points
Manchester United	23	14	7	2	49	27	35
Manchester City	23	13	6	4	45	22	32
Leeds United	23	13	5	5	34	18	31
Sheffield United	23	13	4	6	42	30	30
Derby County	23	11	7	5	39	22	29
Liverpool	23	11	6	6	30	23	28

January 1972

Onwards and Upwards

Saturday 1 January

Derby County v Chelsea

Colin Todd was back in Derby's side for the visit of Chelsea to the Baseball Ground on New Year's Day after recovering from the broken his nose inflicted at Liverpool in December. He had turned out for the reserves against Leeds second string the previous Tuesday. Unfortunately the 1-0 victory that evening was little consolation for the crowd of over 6,000 after the 3-0 defeat at Elland Road a day earlier. Alan Durban also returned to action for the Chelsea match with Hennessey making way.

In an outspoken article on the front page of *The Ram* Brian Clough, who it seemed had been reading the Riot Act, wrote that unless the sharp difference between home and away form was resolved the Rams could end up being an average mid-table side with hopes of Europe shattered completely. 'We are not big enough and we are not strong enough to dish it out when it needs dishing out', he added.

With England international goalkeeper Peter Bonetti out of action for the second match in succession and reserve 'keeper Phillips also injured, Chelsea included 18-year-old Steve Sherwood, their third team 'keeper. In their previous match at home to Ipswich, manager Dave Sexton had staggered the football world by selecting defender David Webb to play in goal and although he had kept a clean sheet in a 2-0 win against Ipswich it had already turned out to be a one-off.

O'Hare hit the crossbar early on but Derby threatened only spasmodically in the first half and when they did young Sherwood showed what a fine prospect he was with his clean handling and excellent positioning for one so inexperienced

After the interval Chelsea's packed defence continued to thwart Derby's below par attack and when the visitors broke forward they did it so quickly that chances always looked likely. Hudson and Kember both went close with efforts that went narrowly wide. It looked as though Derby would have to settle for a goalless stalemate but with just six minutes remaining Gemmill latched on to a pass from Webster before going on a long run. Despite attempts by the Chelsea rear-guard to prevent him shooting, he let fly with a drive which took a deflection off defender David Webb before wrong-footing the unlucky 'keeper and finishing up in the back of the net.

Derby held out for a crucial victory in what had been a hard uncompromising match, with Chelsea's Kember and Hudson booked along with the fiercely competitive Gemmill. Afterwards Peter Osgood said that he thought Chelsea had been the better team and were very unlucky to lose. 'We were never in any trouble at the back', he argued, adding that they had created the better chances, particularly in the second half.

Manchester United, who lost 3-0 at West Ham the same day, hadn't won at all since early December and with City drawing 2-2 at home to lowly Forest, Derby were now back in contention for the title. It was beginning to look as though Leeds might be their biggest obstacle. Revie's men had won 2-0 away at Liverpool and were now only two points behind Manchester United. Derby, therefore, were now in fourth place, two points adrift of Leeds and Manchester City. The big question now was could they conquer their travel-sickness and come away from Southampton seven days later with at least a point but preferably two?

- DERBY COUNTY: Boulton, Webster, Robson, Todd, McFarland, McGovern, Durban, Gemmill, O'Hare, Hector, Hinton.
- CHELSEA: Sherwood, Mulligan, Harris, Hollins, Dempsey, Webb, Garland, Kember, Osgood, Hudson, Houseman. Sub. Cooke for Kember.
- RESULT: Derby County 1 (Gemmill 84), Chelsea 0.
- REFEREE: T. Dawes. • ATTENDANCE: 33,063. • POSITION: 4th.

Saturday 8 January

Southampton v Derby County

In an attempt to rectify Derby's results away from home some supporters had been urging Clough to experiment with a more defensive formation on their travels but the manager thought otherwise and opted for the same side that had overcome Chelsea on New Year's Day for the visit to The Dell. Southampton included the dangerous duo of Mick Channon and Ron Davies up front with England international Terry Paine on the right wing.

There was some surprise when it emerged that Brian Clough was not at the game. Instead he had decided to do some scouting and leave Peter Taylor in charge. Durban went close with a fine shot which scraped the outside of the post early on but before long Southampton were having the best of the exchanges and Gerry O'Brien put them ahead after 13 minutes with his first goal for club.

After that the home side continued to enjoy the bulk of the possession but with McFarland in top form they rarely threatened Boulton. Todd was booked by the referee for obstructing Channon, but with the interval only seconds away the Rams drew level. Efforts from McFarland and Durban had been

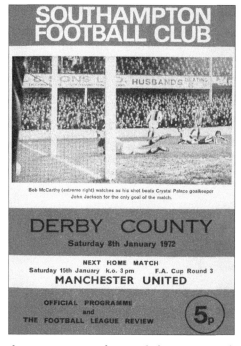

SOUTHAMPTON FOOTBALL CLUB

Bob McCarthy (extreme right) watches as his shot beats Crystal Palace goalkeeper John Jackson for the only goal of the match.

DERBY COUNTY

Saturday 8th January 1972

NEXT HOME MATCH
Saturday 15th January k.o. 3 pm   F.A. Cup Round 3
MANCHESTER UNITED

OFFICIAL PROGRAMME
and
THE FOOTBALL LEAGUE REVIEW

5p

blocked but the ball eventually fell to O'Hare who forced it over the line.

It was the perfect time to equalise and after the interval a more confident Derby began to get a grip on the game. The aerial threat from Channon and Davies was being repelled by the visitors' defence and Southampton began to lose momentum. Although the Rams were becoming increasingly dominant in midfield, most of the fans that had made the long journey to the south coast would probably have settled for a draw after the depressing run of away defeats. But with time running out it was the splendid Robson who surged forward yet again before laying on a chance for Durban who cracked a wonderful 20-yard drive past 'keeper Martin.

It was too late for Southampton to come back and with seconds remaining a frustrated Bobby Stokes was booked by referee Oliver for a bad foul on Gemmill. The end to the match couldn't have been more dramatic but the visitors, who had fought tooth and nail, just about deserved to win.

Later, Peter Taylor said that he thought it was one of Derby's best performances of the season, adding that Boulton would have saved O'Brien's goal if the ball hadn't been diverted off O'Hare. The same afternoon Manchester United lost at home to Wolves, Manchester City drew away at Tottenham and Leeds could only manage a 2-2 draw at home to Ipswich. Those two priceless points had put the Rams right back in the title race, just a couple of points adrift of the leaders.

- SOUTHAMPTON: Martin, McCarthy, Fry, Stokes, Gabriel, Byrne, Paine, Channon, Davies, O'Brien, Jenkins.
- DERBY COUNTY: Boulton, Webster, Robson, Durban, McFarland, Todd, McGovern, Gemmill, O'Hare, Hector, Hinton.
- RESULT: Southampton 1 (O'Brien 13), Derby County 2 (O'Hare 44, Durban 88).
- REFEREE: A. Oliver. • ATTENDANCE: 19, 321. • POSITION: 4th.

Saturday 22 January

West Ham United v Derby County

Derby's first away victory since the end of October at Southampton had lifted spirits enormously. Now they were on their travels again; this time to take on West Ham United at the Boleyn Ground, A relieved Brian Clough opted for the same line-up that had been too good for the Saints. As for the Hammers, manager Ron Greenwood's side included Bobby Moore, Trevor Brooking and Geoff Hurst, who was playing his 400th League game for the club.

Clough was away again, this time looking at a possible signing, leaving Peter Taylor in charge for the second time. The game began at a frantic pace and Derby went ahead as early as the 5th minute. O'Hare started the move, nicking the ball off centre-half Taylor before passing to Hector who found Hinton and the winger fired home past 'keeper Ferguson. The first half was packed with flowing football from both sides and the Rams went close to extending their lead but with half-time approaching Frank Lampard was on the mark to equalise.

It was a disappointing way to end the first period but worse was

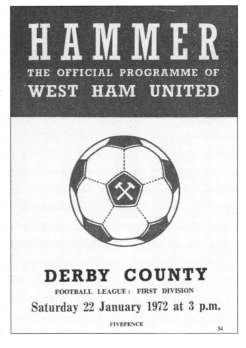

HAMMER

THE OFFICIAL PROGRAMME OF
WEST HAM UNITED

DERBY COUNTY

FOOTBALL LEAGUE: FIRST DIVISION

Saturday 22 January 1972 at 3 p.m.

FIVEPENCE

34

to come two minutes after the restart when the dangerous Pop Robson put the Hammers ahead. McFarland was having yet another outstanding match and it was the central defender pushing forward to head a Hinton corner on to O'Hare. His header was blocked and the ball fell to Durban who scored from close range to make it 2-2. The industrious McGovern was having a field day and Derby appeared to have secured their first draw since early October.

Clyde Best had a goal narrowly ruled out for offside but with just nine minutes remaining Brooking put the home side in front. It was a cruel blow but even then the Rams were not finished and with just three minutes remaining Hector headed home from a Hinton cross at the near post to make it 3-3. It was his first goal since November and a massive relief all round.

Afterwards Peter Taylor praised McFarland who had shored up a strangely hesitant Derby defence which the assistant manager said was making too many errors. 'Roy stood out like a beacon. He's becoming one of the world's best centre-halves,' he added.

The same afternoon Leeds beat Sheffield United 1-0 to go top, level on 36 points with Manchester City who won at Crystal Palace. Manchester United went down at home to Chelsea and were now third, a single point ahead of fourth placed Derby.

- WEST HAM U: Ferguson, McDowell, Lampard, Bonds, Taylor, Moore, Redknapp, Best, Hurst, Brooking, Robson.
- DERBY COUNTY: Boulton, Webster, Robson, Durban, McFarland, Todd, McGovern, Gemmill, O'Hare, Hector, Hinton.
- RESULT: West Ham United 3 (Lampard 43, Robson 47, Brooking 81), Derby County 3 (Hinton 5, Durban 68, Hector 87).
- REFEREE: J. Thacker. • ATTENDANCE: 31,045. • POSITION: 4th.

Saturday 29 January

Derby County v Coventry City

With no new injury concerns Clough stuck with the same side that had come back to force the high scoring draw against West Ham for the home game against Coventry the following Saturday. The Sky Blues who were struggling in the bottom half of the table were becoming something of a bogey team since Derby's return to top-flight football in 1969 having won the two matches at the Baseball Ground and drawn both games at Highfield Road.

The Rams were being frustrated by the well organised Coventry defence in the first half. Although Hector had scored against the Hammers it was his only goal in eight League games and once again he was flitting in and out. The main threat was coming from Hinton on the left wing and in the 20th minute he unleashed a powerful drive which flashed just wide of the post. As for Coventry, their attack was totally lacking penetration although centre-half Blockley went close with a header but he was offside anyway. Although Derby were the better side they were finding it impossible to break the deadlock and it remained scoreless at the interval.

The second half couldn't have started more dramatically. Straight from the kick-off Gemmill picked up a loose pass from Machin and surged forward before playing the ball into the path of Robson who hammered a low cross-shot from 20 yards past 'keeper Glazier to put his side ahead. With the wind behind them Derby looked the more dangerous side going forward and Glazier had to be at his best to save from Hector. Coventry were posing little or no threat to Boulton who was enjoying one of his quietest afternoons of the season.

One effort from Carr sailed over the bar and Rafferty who occasionally managed to ruffle the normally untroubled McFarland should have been booked for a bad foul on the Derby pivot but the referee missed the incident.

Although Todd had been cautioned for retaliation, he had been outstanding once again and afterwards Clough said that he considered that the defender was now ready to play for England. The £170,000 transfer from Sunderland had been considered expensive by some at the time (including chairman Sam Longson), but now it was beginning to look like a bargain.

Although it had not been a particularly entertaining match, the two points lifted Derby up one place to third, two points behind leaders Manchester City who beat Wolves 5-2 and now they were equal on points with second placed Leeds who lost at Tottenham.

As for Manchester United, their 2-1 defeat away to West Brom was their fourth in a row and with three draws on the bounce before that, it had been almost two months since their last win in the League.

- **DERBY COUNTY: Boulton, Webster, Robson, Durban, McFarland Todd, McGovern, Gemmill, O'Hare Hector Hinton.**
- **COVENTRY CITY: Glazier, Smith, Catlin, Machin, Blockley, Parker, Young, Carr, Chilton, Rafferty, Mortimer. Sub: McGuire for Machin.**
- **RESULT: Derby County 1 (Robson 46), Coventry City 0.**
- **REFEREE: H. New. • ATTENDANCE: 29,385. • POSITION: 3rd.**

The main feature in January had been the dramatic slump in the fortunes of Manchester United who had been top at the end December. Leading the pack now were Manchester City but Derby's improved form away from home had enabled them move up to third place.

Early leaders Sheffield United had dropped out of the top six altogether after failing to win a match during the month of January and their 5-0 defeat at Highbury had allowed Arsenal to move up to fifth after two wins and two draws. As for Liverpool, only a comprehensive 4-1 win at home to Crystal Palace saved them from a disastrous month and now they were lying seventh.

Archie Gemmill had been in superb form throughout January. The Scottish international midfielder began the month in just about the best way possible by scoring the late winner against Chelsea on New Year's Day. His penetrating runs and never-say-die attitude were exactly what Derby needed if they were going to get out of a disappointing run of results on their travels and that was exactly what happened a week later when they won at Southampton.

The top of the First Division at the end of January was as follows:

	P	W	D	L	F	A	Points
Manchester City	27	15	8	4	55	28	38
Leeds United	27	15	6	6	39	21	36
Derby County	27	14	8	5	46	26	36
Manchester United	27	14	7	6	51	36	35
Arsenal	27	14	5	8	41	27	33

February 1972

The Challenge Intensifies

Saturday 12 February

Arsenal v Derby County

Two weeks later Derby were in the capital for what was bound to be a difficult match against Arsenal. Sir Alf Ramsey was in the crowd to keep an eye on the likes of McFarland and Todd, as well as Arsenal's Alan Ball and possibly Charlie George too.

The Rams had no serious injury concerns so as usual they were at full strength. Arsenal included future manager George Graham in their line-up as well as their England hopefuls. Both sides put on a fine display of football in the first half although the home side looked more threatening in attack. Charlie

George rattled the post early on and it was the in-form striker who eventually put the Gunners ahead with only seconds remaining in the first half when he headed home past Boulton after Graham had found him with an accurate cross.

After the resumption Durban had a close range effort blocked and McFarland was unlucky to see his shot go narrowly wide after running through to collect a pass from Hector. Boulton was at the top of his game making fine saves from Ball and George but McFarland and Todd were in top form too and must have impressed the England manager.

Arsenal continued to look the more threatening going forward and with six minutes remaining George put the game beyond Derby's reach from the penalty spot. Webster had appeared to be pushed in the back by Kennedy but referee Burns ignored the incident and there even seemed to be a hint of offside when George burst through and rounded 'keeper Boulton. The 'keeper opted to pull him down just as he was about to shoot. The referee blew for a penalty and George himself fired home from the spot.

In the end the Gunners just about deserved their victory if only because they posed the greater threat up front. After the match Clough was particularly com-

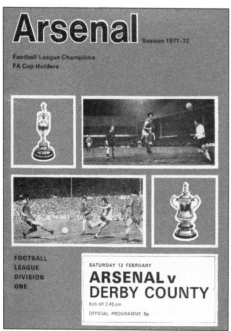

plimentary about Charlie George who he said had scored a marvellous goal and deserved to be on the winning side. No wonder some Derby fans were thinking that he was just the sort of player Clough needed.

The win took Arsenal up to fourth place, just a point behind Derby. They had now gone 12 games unbeaten and were beginning to emerge as serious challengers for the title. But with leaders Manchester City and second-placed Leeds both drawing the Rams were still very much in contention too.

- ARSENAL: Wilson, Rice, Nelson, Kelly, McLintock, Simpson, Armstrong, Ball, George, Kennedy, Graham.
- DERBY COUNTY: Boulton, Webster, Robson, Durban, McFarland, Todd, McGovern, Gemmill, O'Hare, Hector, Hinton.
- RESULT: Arsenal 2 (George 44, 84 pen), Derby County 0.
- REFEREE: K. Burns. • ATTENDANCE: 52,055. • POSITION: 3rd.

Saturday 19 February

Derby County v Nottingham Forest

Although the 2-0 reversal at Highbury had highlighted some weaknesses in Clough's squad, particularly their inability to find the back of the net regularly enough, hopes were high that they could bounce back against their increasingly bitter rivals from Nottingham.

Despite the recent lack of goals the manager opted for an unchanged line-up for the sixth match in a row. Surely it was only a matter of time before Hector rediscovered his touch and Hinton was almost certain to be up for it against his old club. Forest included winger Ian Storey-Moore in their side with Martin O'Neill returning in attack after a five-match absence.

Derby had the better of the early exchanges and Hector was instrumental in their first goal. It came to eleven minutes before the interval when his clever pass inside the full-back was seized upon by Hinton who placed a sublime lob over Barron who had been expecting a cross. Four minutes later Forest's Paul Richardson was dispossessed by the industrious McGovern who then found O'Hare and the centre-forward placed the ball past the 'keeper into the back of the net. It was a superb effort by the centre-forward.

Hinton was having a field day against the club who had once boasted that they had been glad to get rid of him and four minutes into the second half he was on the mark again to make it 3-0 after the cumbersome Hindley had fouled O'Hare on the edge of the box. Instead of unleashing one of his specials, Hinton opted to chip the ball over the stranded Barron and just under the cross-bar.

Storey-Moore looked dangerous at times and on one occasion Boulton had to be at his bravest, diving at his feet to deny what looked like a certain goal.

Forest were unable to pose any other threat to the impressive Derby rear-guard and when a clearance fell to Hector their abject defence allowed him to run through before firing past the 'keeper into the corner of the net to make it 4-0. Shortly afterwards he came close to adding a second but his shot came back off the woodwork.

It was a relief to see such an excellent player as Hector returning to form in front of goal. Rumours of new faces arriving at the Baseball Ground to boost Derby's striking force would probably go away now. In any case, with attendances nowhere near the 40,000 that they were attracting two years earlier, a slightly frustrated Brian Clough had made it clear that they weren't in the same League as the big city clubs when it came to bringing in expensive players.

After the match, while some Forest players were bemoaning the state of the pitch, Clough was of the opinion that it had all been too embarrassing. The victory which had enabled the Rams to complete a comprehensive double over their neighbours had been a particularly comfortable one and in McGovern, Derby had the best player on view.

But for some careless finishing late on the score line could have been even more embarrassing for Matt Gillies, the beleaguered Forest manager. His side had struggled to get out of their own half for most of the game and had never troubled the Derby defence, so much so that McFarland and Todd were often able to push forward into midfield. Afterwards some pundits were of the opinion that the shambolic Forest outfit was the worst side to visit the Baseball Ground in the League all season and were odds-on for a spell in the Second Division.

- **DERBY COUNTY: Boulton, Webster, Robson, Durban, McFarland, Todd, McGovern, Gemmill, O'Hare, Hector, Hinton.**
- **NOTTINGHAM F: Barron, Gemmill, Winfield, Chapman, Hindley, Cottam, Lyons, O'Neill, Cormack, Richardson. Storey-Moore.**
- **RESULT: Derby County 4 (Hinton 34, 49, O'Hare 38, Hector 63), Nottingham Forest 0.**
- **REFEREE: R. Matthewson. • ATTENDANCE: 31,801. • POSITION: 3rd.**

Derby had been restricted to just two League games in February after making progress in the FA Cup. The disappointing defeat at Arsenal had been followed by the thumping of Forest but this was enough to keep them hanging on to third place three points behind leaders Manchester City and a single point adrift of second placed Leeds. Hot on the Rams' tails were Liverpool who were bouncing back after winning their three fixtures and Arsenal who had picked up maximum points from their two, including the 2-0 win against Derby, were still in the frame.

Alan Durban, one of only a handful of players to survive Clough's initial cull four years earlier, had by now become an even better player under the new manager. No one had played better than the Welsh international in February. His clever positional play, passing ability and an uncanny knack of being in the right place at the right time to score vital goals had made him an extremely valuable member of the team.

The top of the First Division table at the end of February was as follows:

	P	W	D	L	F	A	Points
Manchester City	30	16	9	5	59	34	41
Leeds United	29	16	7	6	44	22	39
Derby County	29	15	8	6	50	28	38
Liverpool	30	15	7	8	40	27	37
Arsenal	29	16	5	8	44	27	37
Wolverhampton W	30	13	10	7	50	42	36
Tottenham H	29	13	9	7	45	31	35

March 1972

Five Wins and a Draw

Saturday 4 March

Derby County v Wolverhampton Wanderers

Derby were unchanged yet again for the home match against Wolves at the beginning of March. By now supporters had become accustomed to seeing the same 11 players week-in, week-out but it was only possible because of their fitness and desire to play and maybe a bit of luck with injuries. The notorious Baseball Ground mud might have been difficult for visiting teams to cope with but Derby had to contend with it every other week.

Before the match got underway at a packed stadium Derby unveiled Ian Storey-Moore as their new signing to rapturous applause. Unfortunately it was about to become a particularly embarrassing episode when Forest refused to sanction his move and he opted to join Manchester United instead.

The Rams began sluggishly on a wet afternoon and it was Wolves who went ahead from the penalty-spot in the seventh minute through Jim McCalliog after Boulton had up-ended Derek Dougan. The first half was becoming an increasingly frenetic affair with the away side determined to hold on to their lead by every means at their disposal. Despite being on top for long periods Derby were unable to find a way through and it remained 1-0 to Bill McGarry's side at half-time.

Five minutes after the interval the referee pointed to the spot for the second time after Munro had tackled Hector from behind and Hinton who had rattled the bar in the first half made no mistake from 12 yards, sending 'keeper Parkes the wrong way. It was his 14th goal of the season and the seventh from penalties.

Derby were looking the more likely to take the lead and there was just under 20 minutes remaining when McFarland moved upfield to soar above the Wolves' defence and head Hinton's free-kick past 'keeper Parkes to make it 2-1. There was no way back for Wolves after that. They were missing the influence of Bailey in midfield and despite a late rally were unable to force an equaliser.

The two points maintained Derby's position in third place behind leaders Manchester City and second place behind Leeds although the Rams had played at least one game less than their main competitors.

- DERBY COUNTY: Boulton, Webster, Robson, Durban, McFarland, Todd, McGovern, Gemmill, O'Hare, Hector, Hinton.
- WOLVES: Parkes, Shaw, Taylor, Hegan, Munro, McAlle, McCalliog, Hibbitt, Richards, Dougan, Wagstaffe.
- RESULT: Derby County 2 (Hinton 50 pen, McFarland 71), Wolves 1 (McCalliog 7 pen).
- REFEREE: R. Challis. • ATTENDANCE: 33,456. • POSITION: 3rd.

Saturday 11 March

Tottenham Hotspur v Derby County

The narrow victory at home to Wolves was followed by a tricky away fixture with Spurs a week later. Derby had been unchanged since the end of December but with Durban now out of contention after picking up an injury, in came Terry Hennessey for his first appearance since the defeat at Leeds just after Christmas.

The Rams had not won at White Hart Lane since the 1933-34 season and with Spurs enjoying a formidable record at home this season (only West Ham had come away with both points), no one expected them to roll over. Chances were few and far between in a disappointing first half with Derby, if anything, looking slightly more threatening than Bill Nicholson's men. Although the home side had created very little in front of goal they did come close on one occasion but the ball was eventually cleared after a frantic scramble in the six-yard box.

Hennessey was making an encouraging return to first team action after his lengthy absence. At his best the Welsh international was a magnificent player and it was unfortunate that his career with the Rams was still being hampered by fitness concerns.

It remained scoreless at the inter-val and although a couple of Martin Chivers headers went close the Rams rear-guard was generally coping well against the powerful striker. So far Spurs' only other threat had come from a Martin Peters shot and Alan Gilzean had been well marshalled by the excellent McFarland.

With defences generally on top in the second half neither side looked likely to break the deadlock and it was looking increasingly likely that the game would end goalless. Derby would probably have settled for a

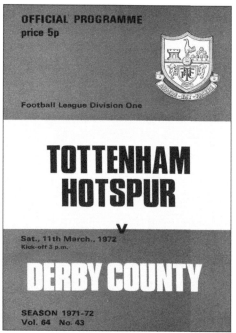

OFFICIAL PROGRAMME
price 5p

Football League Division One

TOTTENHAM HOTSPUR
v
Sat., 11th March., 1972
Kick-off 3 p.m.

DERBY COUNTY

SEASON 1971-72
Vol. 64 No. 43

point and Kevin Hector was cautioned by referee Morrisey for time-wasting five minutes from the end.

Seconds later Spurs were having difficulty in clearing the ball upfield after a Derby corner. Mike England attempted to pass the ball back to Jennings but unfortunately for him the 'keeper had moved too close and he was unable to hold on to it. Hector pounced and Jennings had no alternative than to pull him down in the box.

It was a clear penalty and although Jennings guessed the right way he was unable to prevent Hinton's spot kick from finding the corner of the net despite a despairing dive. It was the penalty specialist's 15th goal of the season but none had been more valuable than this one.

The two priceless points meant Derby remained in third place and very much in contention because although they were five points behind leaders Manchester City who won 2-1 at Everton, they had two games in hand. Leeds beat Coventry 1-0 at Elland Road to remain second, one point clear of the Rams. Fourth placed Liverpool could only manage a draw at Chelsea and were just two points further back although they had played a game more.

- TOTTENHAM H: Jennings, Evans, Knowles, Holder, England, Beal, Gilzean, Perryman, Chivers, Peters, Morgan.
- DERBY COUNTY: Boulton, Webster, Robson, Hennessey, McFarland, Todd, McGovern, Gemmill, O'Hare, Hector, Hinton.
- RESULT: Tottenham Hotspur 0, Derby County 1 (Hinton 86 pen).
- REFEREE: A. Morrisey. • ATTENDANCE: 36,310. • POSITION: 3rd.

Saturday 18 March

Derby County v Leicester City

The following Saturday Leicester provided the opposition at the Baseball Ground. With Hinton unavailable because of a hamstring injury, Gemmill was handed the number 11 shirt and Hennessey was in midfield wearing number eight. The Foxes' brilliant young 'keeper Peter Shilton was out of their side through injury for the second match in succession and in his place was the inexperienced Mark Wallington. Derby started brightly and intense pressure on the Leicester goal was rewarded in the 17th minute when O'Hare latched on to a fine pass from Durban and shrugged off a challenge by Whitworth before clipping the ball over Wallington into the back of the net. After that the home side looked increasingly comfortable and it seemed only a matter of time before they increased their lead but the visitors, to their credit, managed to hold out until half-time.

Walker came on for Hennessey in the 64th minute allowing Gemmill to revert to his normal position in midfield and three minutes later the substitute floated over a corner kick and Durban ghosted in at the near post to head past Wallington and double Derby's lead.

David Nish was playing particularly well at left-back and it was beginning to look as though the Rams would have to settle for the two goals but with time running out Gemmill got his head to a Leicester throw-in. The ball fell to Hector near the halfway line and he surged through the visitors' defence shrugging off a challenge from Cross before beating Wallington with an accurate cross shot into the far corner to make it 3-0. It was a magnificent effort by the striker who was approaching his best form at a crucial stage of the season.

This was Derby's 10th home win in succession and afterwards an upbeat Brian Clough said that his side must continue to fight hard if they were going to challenge for the title.

With Leeds in FA Cup action, Derby's 3-0 victory lifted them into second place behind leaders Manchester City who beat Chelsea 1-0 at Maine Road and although they were still five points adrift of City they had two games in hand. Liverpool thrashed Newcastle 5-0 and were still very much in contention too.

- **DERBY COUNTY: Boulton, Webster, Robson, Durban, McFarland, Todd, McGovern, Hennessey, O'Hare, Hector, Gemmill. Sub. Walker for Hennessey.**
- **LEICESTER CITY: Wallington, Whitworth, Nish, Cross, Manley, Woollett, Fern, Sammels, Weller, Birchenall, Glover. Sub. Lee for Fern.**
- **RESULT: Derby County 3 (O'Hare 17, Durban 67, Hector 86), Leicester City 0.**
- **REFEREE: V. James. • ATTENDANCE: 34,019. • POSITION: 2nd.**

Wednesday 22 March

Derby County v Ipswich Town

Four days later middle-of-the-table Ipswich Town were Derby's opponents at the Baseball Ground for another crucial fixture. Back in Clough's line-up came Hinton who had recovered from the hamstring injury that had kept him out of the Leicester match with Hennessey making way. Viljoen was unavailable for Ipswich and manager Bobby Robson sprang a surprise by switching right-back Mick Mills to centre-forward with Hammond replacing him in defence.

It was extremely disappointing to see the Baseball Ground far from full after the splendid victory over Leicester and the attendance of fewer than 27,000 was the lowest of the season so far. On a hard bouncy surface Derby had the best of the early exchanges but it soon became clear that Ipswich were going to pack their defence in an attempt to stifle Derby's attack which had been so impressive against the Foxes.

The game was just 15 minutes old when a long clearance from Boulton bounced over two defenders allowing the alert Hector to run past both of them before planting a sublime volley past 'keeper Hammond. It was a second goal in successive matches by the striker but five minutes later Hinton who had been struggling with an injury had to leave the field and was replaced by Walker.

At times Ipswich had as many as eight men behind the ball as they tried to prevent a second goal. Derby seemed reluctant to throw too many players forward in case they were caught out on the break although their splendid defence, ably marshalled by McFarland, seemed capable of snuffing out the occasional threat and Boulton was rarely troubled.

In the end it was the result that mattered and although supporters would have preferred a more exciting contest, the majority were happy enough with another two points. The state of the Baseball Ground playing surface hadn't helped but Derby had coped with it better than the opposition. On the same evening Leeds could only muster a 0-0 draw at Leicester and with Manchester City not playing, the Rams moved to within three points of the leaders with a game in hand.

- DERBY COUNTY: Boulton, Webster, Robson, Durban, McFarland Todd, McGovern, Gemmill, O'Hare, Hector, Hinton. Sub. Walker for Hinton.
- IPSWICH TOWN: Best, Hammond, Harper, Morris, Hunter, Jefferson, Robertson, Miller, Mills, Belfitt, Whymark. Sub. Lambert for Belfitt.
- RESULT: Derby County 1 (Hector 15), Ipswich Town 0.
- REFEREE: E. Wallace. • ATTENDANCE: 26,738. • POSITION: 2nd.

Saturday 25 March

Stoke City v Derby County

After five consecutive victories in the League the Rams and their supporters were in a buoyant mood for their visit to Stoke City's Victoria Ground. With Hinton out through injury in came Walker for his first start of the season. Although he had proved a capable deputy on his three appearances as a substitute, Hinton had been in prime form and would almost certainly be missed, both for his goals and his crossing ability.

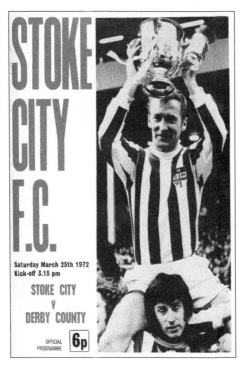

Tony Waddington's side included England 'keeper Gordon Banks and making a rare appearance was the brilliant, if unpredictable, George Eastham. Waddington had the knack of recruiting players who were slightly past their peak and then getting the best out of them and Eastham, who had starred at Newcastle and Arsenal, was a fine example.

The referee was the eccentric Roger Kirkpatrick and that afternoon he was destined to make a controversial decision in the dying minutes that would determine the result of the match. In front of a near capacity crowd, which included a large contingent from the East Midlands, there was little to choose between the two sides in a fiercely contested first half. Although Derby created the best chances, both goalkeepers were in fine form and the game remained goalless at the interval.

Stoke were awarded a penalty shortly after the resumption when Todd brought down the dangerous Harry Burrows in the area and Jimmy Greenhoff, beat Boulton with the spot-kick to put his side ahead. Derby began to push forward for the equaliser and three minutes later Durban launched a free-kick from just outside the area which swerved round the wall, past Banks and into the back of the net. It was an outstanding effort by a player who was back to his very best.

The goal had the effect of spurring on Clough's side who continued to push hard for the winner and with time running out Hector appeared to have given his side a well-deserved victory only for referee Kirkpatrick to disallow what seemed a perfectly good goal. Afterwards Clough, as usual, refused to condemn the official but suggested that reporters should ask the ref to explain his decision. Kirkpatrick said that he considered that Hector had elbowed Banks but the Derby striker later insisted that he had made no contact whatsoever with the 'keeper.

Although an away draw was welcome enough, it seemed more like a point lost than a point won, particularly as Leeds had beaten Arsenal 3-0 although Manchester City had only managed a draw at Newcastle. Fourth placed Liverpool who won at Southampton were still in contention too. It was beginning to look as though it would go right to the wire.

- STOKE CITY: Banks, Marsh, Jump, Bernard, Smith, Bloor, Conroy, Greenhoff, Ritchie, Eastham, Burrows. Sub: Skeels for Eastham.
- DERBY COUNTY: Boulton, Webster, Robson, Durban, McFarland, Todd, McGovern, Gemmill, O'Hare, Hector, Walker.
- RESULT: Stoke City 1 (Greenhoff 48 pen), Derby County 1 (Durban 51).
- REFEREE: R. Kirkpatrick. • ATTENDANCE: 38,238. • POSITION: 2nd.

Tuesday 28 March

Crystal Palace v Derby County

Derby County supporters making the journey to the capital three days later for a Tuesday evening fixture against Crystal Palace under the Selhurst Park floodlights were still bemoaning Hector's disallowed goal at the Victoria Ground on the Saturday. A victory against Bert Head's side would now be extremely welcome; particularly with a crucial home fixture with Leeds coming up the following weekend.

With the injured Hinton still out of action, Walker continued to fill in on the left wing. Signed by Clough from non-League Northwich Victoria in February 1968, he was still proving to be a useful member of the manager's small squad. Hinton had become virtually irreplaceable and Walker's opportunities had become increasingly few and far between but that afternoon he was about to show why Clough had stuck with him.

Also in the Derby side replacing the injured McGovern was Hennessey for

Football League Division One
Tuesday 28 March 1972
Crystal Palace v Derby County   Price 6p

only his 17th League game of the season. As for Palace who were struggling in the lower reaches of the First Division, their line-up included winger Peter Taylor and the ex-Chelsea forward Bobby Tambling.

It was soon apparent that the Rams were back to somewhere near their best. Playing some delightful football they should have gone ahead on the quarter hour mark after being awarded a penalty when O'Hare was felled in the box but with Hinton missing Gemmill accepted the responsibility for the spot-kick only to fire wide.

Derby had conceded a miserly four goals in their previous eight matches so it wasn't surprising that when Palace did push forward they were finding it impossible to break down the visitors' rearguard in which Todd and Robson were outstanding.

The Rams continued to press for the opener and it duly arrived in the 34th minute when Walker fired past 'keeper John Jackson from close range after finding himself with space in front of goal following a corner. Despite going close minutes later they had to settle for a 1-0 score line at the interval.

The second half began with the Palace on the defensive but Derby were still having trouble turning territorial advantage into goals and in the end were happy to settle for the narrow victory. Clough thought that although his side had missed McGovern and Hinton they had acquitted themselves better than Palace.

Derby were now within a single point of leaders Manchester City. Worryingly though, Leeds had thrashed relegation candidates Nottingham Forest 6-1 the previous evening and were only a further point behind in third place and had played a game less. The fixture between Clough's increasingly confident side and Revie's side four days later on Easter Monday couldn't come quickly enough.

- **CRYSTAL PALACE: Jackson, Payne, Goodwin, Kellard, McCormick, Bell, Craven, Queen, Wallace, Taylor, Tambling. Sub: Wall for Tambling.**
- **DERBY COUNTY: Boulton, Webster, Robson, Durban, McFarland, Todd, Hennessey, Gemmill, O'Hare, Hector, Walker.**
- **RESULT: Crystal Palace 0, Derby County 1 (Walker 34).**
- **REFEREE: C. Nicholls. • ATTENDANCE: 21,158. • POSITION: 2nd.**

By now Colin Boulton was regarded as one the best goalkeepers in the country thanks to his sheer consistency and March had been another fine month for a player who had waited so long to make the position his own. He had conceded just two goals in the six League games and both of those had come from the penalty spot even if it was the 'keeper himself who had felt it necessary to haul down Wolves' Derek Dougan for one of them. Earlier in the season the Rams had snapped up Graham Moseley, a promising young 'keeper from Blackburn, and he had been putting in a series of excellent performances for the reserve side. It was no bad thing to have someone pushing the number one 'keeper, but Boulton had no intention of surrendering his place.

March had been a magnificent month for Derby in the League with their five wins and a draw. By now Manchester United had dropped out of the top six altogether after losing both of their matches and had lost six games in a row. Manchester City with four wins and a draw in the month were top of the table ahead of Leeds who had won four, drawn two and were looking particularly dangerous They had beaten Manchester United 5-1 at the end of February and then began the month of March with an awesome 7-0 annihilation of Southampton followed later by the 6-1 thumping of Forest. Although Liverpool were three points behind Derby, their four victories had included a 4-0 win against Everton before beating Newcastle 5-0, so they were still very much in contention too.

With Leeds drawing at West Ham three days later on Friday 31 March the top of the First Division table at the end of the month looked like this:

	P	W	D	L	F	A	Points
Manchester City	35	20	10	5	66	36	50
Leeds United	35	20	9	6	61	22	49
Derby County	35	20	9	6	59	30	49
Liverpool	35	19	8	8	52	28	46
Wolverhampton W	34	15	11	8	57	47	41
Tottenham H	34	15	11	8	51	34	41

John O'Hare in action at the Baseball Ground in the crucial 2-0 victory over title rivals Leeds United on 1 April.

April 1972

Closing In

Saturday 1 April

Derby County v Leeds United

The football fixtures over Easter would probably go a long way to determining the eventual destination of the First Division trophy. With Hinton still recovering from injury, Walker continued on the left wing for the Rams and Leeds included the versatile Paul Madeley at centre-forward in place of Mick Jones. Don Revie had intimated earlier that Johnny Giles would be missing because of a strain but there he was running out with the rest of the team at five minutes to three. Almost exactly two years earlier Revie had staggered everyone at a packed Baseball Ground by selecting a reserve side for an important First

the Ram

7p

Official Newspaper of
Derby County F.C.

No. 27 (v. Leeds United, April 1, 1972)

An Easter egg filled with Championship points

> ...intrude on private grief. If this lot win the League, I'll eat this match report on toast.

One chap who'll be looking with more than normal interest at the Derby-Leeds result will be SUN sportswriter, Frank Clough, who wrote the bit above in his report of Rams' 1-nil defeat at Manchester United on October 16. WE COULD BE SEEING YOU CHEWING IT ON TOAST YET, FRANK OLD SON!

CHEER RAMS
TO THE TOP

An Easter egg full of good wishes to all our readers from the Miss Derby Ram... and an Easter egg chock full of Championship points, is her wish to the Derby County team and management. And so say all of us!

HINTON: CROSSED FINGERS

RAMS ARE STILL hoping leading scorer Alan Hinton will be fit to face Leeds United, first due to play at West Ham on Good Friday, in the vital Championship match at the Baseball Ground on Saturday.

Hinton missed the games at Stoke and Palace with a leg strain. Saturday's all-ticket game is the start of a tough run—four games in eight days. Newcastle are here on Monday, then Rams go to Albion on Wednesday (7.30) and Sheffield United the following Saturday.

The Ramaway will run to both away games leaving for West Brom at 5.30 and picking up at Burton at 5.44 (return fare 70p). Tickets at £1 and 80p are available from Albion. Sheffield have 80p and 55p seats for sale.

26,738
Were you missing?

A CERTAIN FULL HOUSE at the Baseball Ground, for the star attraction against Leeds United, will not take the worried frowns off the faces of Derby County officials.

THEY CAN'T FORGET THAT ONLY 26,738 PEOPLE TURNED UP FOR THE WEDNESDAY NIGHT GAME AGAINST IPSWICH TOWN LAST WEEK.

It was the lowest gate of the season.

How come, at a time like this, when the team is in there with a real title chance, the gate drops to almost 6,000 below the 32,000 average.

That figure is already 8,000 below the 40,000 attendances desperately needed if Derby County are to have the cash to keep them among the country's top clubs.

● Comments Brian Clough: 'It's depressing when the team is doing so well. There must be a reason the town is turning its back on us. But what is it?'

● Confirms club secretary, Mr. Stuart Webb: 'Income of this sort from the gate just isn't enough to do the sort of things the public expect from us.'

The Secretary pointed out that Leicester (playing Leeds), Stoke (against Manchester United) and Notts were all playing on the same night. 'It all added up to 3,000 plus off our gate,' he felt. 'Thank goodness we don't often get close-by counter-attractions of that sort very often.'

● POINTS OUT Chairman, Mr. Sam Longson, the man who, with his Board colleagues, has dipped deep in his pockets to underwrite the club's bank balance: 'A gate like this, at this time especially, is depressing.'

● CHALLENGES skipper Roy McFarland: 'Don't they want a top team in Derby?'

OVER TO YOU, THE MISSING SUPPORTERS. LEEDS AND MANCHESTER CITY FANS UNDER THE HAMMER, TOO. TURN TO PAGE 9.

The Ram The Ram The Ram The Ram The Ram The

DERBY COUNTY

The Ram ... am The
The Ram **23** am The
The Ram ... am The
The Ram The Ram The
The Ram The Ram The

Voucher

Who is the new keeper?

Keeping goal during a practice game is French international star Sacha Distel, who joined Rams in training while he was starring at the Talk of the Midlands a few days ago. See other pictures, page 3 and page 7.

INDUSTRIAL PROBLEMS ———

INDUSTRIAL problems nationally in the printing industry may lead to some enforced cuts on our usual standards for this edition. We apologise, and trust you will bear with us.

And we are sorry for not having four colour pictures in this issue

BILLY BREMNER... great Leeds United star.

Division match. His argument was that this would allow him to field a full-strength line-up for a European Cup semi-final against Celtic two days later. Derby had cruised to a 4-1 victory and Leeds were fined by the FA for their actions which were deemed to be totally disrespectful to the paying public as well as the Football League. Their ploy didn't work anyway, Celtic winning 1-0 at Elland Road on their way to the final. Revie wasn't making the same mistake this time.

The game got underway in a frenetic atmosphere at a Baseball Ground bursting at the seams and there were only five minutes on the clock when McGovern was booked by referee Smith for clattering into Giles. Leeds had the ball in the net shortly afterwards but Eddie Gray's effort was disallowed for offside.

Derby were soon enjoying the better of the exchanges with Hector in sparkling form. McGovern, undeterred by his early booking, was keeping Giles quiet and the Rams nearly went ahead when a fine effort by Gemmill was headed off the line by full-back Reaney.

O'Hare was also having an excellent afternoon and it was the centre-forward who opened the scoring in the 16th minute heading Durban's accurate centre past 'keeper Sprake. It was a marvellous way for the Scottish international to mark his 200th League appearance for the Rams.

After that Leeds had no answer to the rampant Derby attack with Hector and O'Hare both going close. McFarland was finding time to join in too and he was unlucky not to extend the lead with a splendid effort. Although it remained 1-0 at the interval it was only a matter of time before the Rams added a second and when Hector opened up the Leeds defence with a superb angled pass, O'Hare seemed certain to score. Sprake blocked his goal-bound shot and the ball broke to Hunter who could only watch in agony as it rebounded off him and into the back of the net to make it 2-0.

After that only some heroic defending by Leeds prevented Derby from running riot. Under continual pressure Revie's men could muster only the occasional attack and when they did the home side's defence marshalled by McFarland quickly stubbed out any threat and Boulton in goal was rarely troubled.

Brian Clough was delighted with the victory. 'We have played the Derby way,' he said afterwards and even Revie had to admit that Derby had been magnificent and were full value for their win before tipping Clough's side for the title if they weren't able to win it themselves.

With leaders Manchester City losing 2-1 at home to Stoke on the same afternoon the two points lifted Derby to the top of the table. But with dark-horses Liverpool winning at home to West Brom, the title race was still wide open, particularly as the Rams were due to take on the Reds at the Baseball Ground in the last match of the season. But that was exactly a month away and a lot could happen before that.

- DERBY COUNTY: Boulton, Webster, Robson, Durban, McFarland, Todd, McGovern, Gemmill, O'Hare, Hector, Walker.
- LEEDS UNITED: Sprake, Reaney, Cooper, Bremner, Charlton, Hunter, Lorimer, Clarke, Madeley, Giles, Gray.
- RESULT: Derby County 2 (O'Hare 16, Hunter 69 og), Leeds United 0.
- REFEREE: D. Smith. • ATTENDANCE: 38,611. • POSITION: 1st.

Monday 3 April

Derby County v Newcastle United

Although Derby had outplayed Leeds on the Saturday to go top, most pundits were still making Clough's side outsiders for the title, a view reinforced by the bookies. Manchester City were still fancied too but had recently signed the unpredictable Rodney Marsh from QPR and there were rumours that his arrival had started to destabilise their squad.

Two days after the thriller against Leeds the Baseball Ground was packed for the second time for the visit of mid-table Newcastle United. Although Walker had not let the side down there was relief all round when it was discovered that Hinton had recovered from injury and would resume on the left wing after a three-match absence. On the face of it Newcastle who had lost 1-0 at Sheffield United on the Saturday had little to play for.

Although the Rams attacked from the kick-off they were soon discovering that the hard-working Newcastle defence was going to be difficult to break down. Boulton, who had been playing with an injured finger for a few weeks, was being well protected by his defenders but there were fears that it might not be Derby's day when McFarland went down injured following a mid-air collision with Tommy Gibb. He had been keeping the prolific Malcolm Macdonald relatively quiet until then and fortunately the Newcastle striker was unable to capitalise on the centre-half's absence for treatment.

It remained scoreless at half-time and when Gibb was taken off on a stretcher suffering from concussion early in the second half, on came substitute Cassidy to replace him. Boulton was forced into making saves from Green and Macdonald and it was looking increasingly likely that the match would end scoreless. But with 20 minutes remaining the nippy Barrowclough was felled by McFarland who had been playing on with his head bandaged. The resultant free-kick was not properly cleared and it was substitute Cassidy in the right place at the right time to fire coolly past Boulton.

Despite frantic efforts, Derby were unable find a way through the determined Newcastle rearguard and the match ended in an extremely disappointing 1-0 defeat. It was a bitter blow and a totally unexpected one too. Supporters had been anticipating that the end-of-season fixtures against Manchester City and Liverpool were likely to be particularly tricky but this had been put down as a home banker. Afterwards a deflated Brian Clough admitted that his side just couldn't break down the Newcastle defence in which he said Moncur deserved full marks.

Leeds and Manchester City were not playing that afternoon but, worryingly, Liverpool beat Manchester United 3-0 at Old Trafford and were now serious contenders for the title. The following day Manchester City lost 2-0 at Southampton and now, rather like their neighbours from Old Trafford, they appeared to be on the slide too.

- DERBY COUNTY: Boulton, Webster, Robson, Durban, McFarland, Todd, McGovern, Gemmill, O'Hare, Hector, Hinton.
- NEWCASTLE U: McFaul, Craig, Clark, Gibb, Howard, Moncur, Barrowclough, Green, Macdonald, Tudor, Reid. Sub. Cassidy for Gibb.
- RESULT: Derby County 0, Newcastle United 1 (Cassidy 71).
- REFEREE: R. Tinkler. • ATTENDANCE: 38,119. • POSITION: 1st.

Wednesday 5 April

West Bromwich Albion v Derby County

Two days later Derby were off to the Hawthorns to take on West Bromwich Albion. Although it was the third match in five days, Clough decided to stick with the same XI that had struggled against Newcastle. No doubt he would have liked to freshen up his side but he had little option other than to keep faith with the men who had performed so well throughout most of the season. West Brom included the promising Asa Hartford in midfield with the dangerous duo of Tony Brown and Jeff Astle up front.

Although the Rams were playing their usual cultured brand of football in the first half they were finding it difficult to find a way through the Baggies' resolute defence in which centre-half Wile was outstanding. The home side preferred the long ball style of play allied to a more physical approach and although they did trouble the Rams' rearguard once or twice there was no way past the superb Boulton.

Gemmill linked up well with Durban but then failed to capitalise in front of goal and Durban himself could only muster a weak header from McGovern's centre. Hector then shot wide after Robertson, who was about to attempt a back-pass, failed to notice him.

Later, Hector had a powerful volley blocked by Suggett but arguably the best chance of a disappointing contest fell to Durban following a Webster cross. Rising unchallenged on the edge of the six-yard box, he was unable to get his header on target and although West Brom rallied late on the match ended goalless.

Clough thought that Derby were beginning to look jaded. 'There were a lot of tired legs out there', he said, 'but we will keep plugging away'. The lack of goals (five in the last six matches including an own goal) was becoming a matter of concern again.

- WEST BROM A: Osborne, Nisbet, Wilson, Suggett, Wile, Robertson, Hope, Brown T., Astle, Brown A., Hartford.
- DERBY COUNTY: Boulton, Webster, Robson, Durban, McFarland, Todd, McGovern, Gemmill, O'Hare, Hector, Hinton.
- RESULT: West Bromwich Albion 0, Derby County 0.
- REFEREE: R. Challis. • ATTENDANCE: • 32,439. • POSITION: 1st.

Saturday 8 April

Sheffield United v Derby County

Although the goalless draw at the Hawthorns on the Wednesday had been enough to keep the Rams top of the table, if they were going to lift the First Division trophy they would have to start scoring goals again.

Sheffield United had enjoyed a fabulous start to the season. At the end of September they had been top of the League, winning eight of their first 10 games and drawing the other two. It couldn't last and when they came to the Baseball Ground towards the end of November Derby had beaten them 3-0 in a totally one-sided game. Five months later, there were indications that the Blades were beginning rediscover their early season form. They had beaten Newcastle and drawn with Manchester United over the Easter period, so doing the double over the Yorkshire outfit wasn't likely to be straightforward. Although Derby's results and performances in their last two matches had been disappointing, Clough opted for an unchanged side yet again for the visit to Bramall Lane. The home side stuck with the same XI that had drawn 1-1 with Manchester United.

The Blades looked the more confident of the two sides early on and the Rams were soon struggling to cope with a series of attacks. Scullion went close to opening the scoring and when Gemmill put Derby ahead in the 12th minute it was very much against the run of play.

Six minutes later Hinton floated over a corner from the right and when Durban and Bobby Hope challenged for it in mid-air the ball rebounded off Mackenzie before finishing up in the back of the net. Afterwards it transpired that Durban had got a touch and he was credited with the goal. The two set-backs had shocked United who soon began to fade and Derby were unlucky not to go into the half-time break with a bigger lead after playing some fine attacking football.

Twenty minutes after the resumption Hector made it 3-0 with a neat near-post header from yet another Hinton cross. It was the back-to-form striker's 200th goal in League football. Nine minutes later O'Hare completed the rout by adding a fourth. His goal, arguably the best of the lot, came after a short corner which was followed by some clever play on the edge of the box and when the ball eventually came to the centre-forward he evaded a challenge, swivelled cleverly, and rifled an accurate shot into the far corner.

The 4-0 victory took Derby's points total up to 54. It was their biggest away win in the three seasons since returning to the First Division but Clough, although happy with the four goal victory, thought that they could have doubled it.

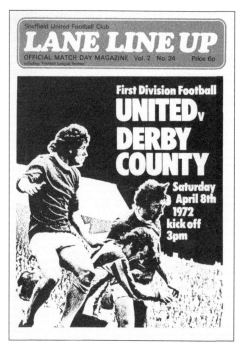

The same afternoon Leeds beat Stoke 3-0 at Elland Road, Manchester City overcame West Ham 3-1 at home and a packed Anfield saw Liverpool, dark horses for the title, win 3-1 against Coventry City. It was beginning to look as though it would all depend on Derby's last two games of the season away at Manchester City's Maine Road and at home to Liverpool on 1 May. But before then there was the little matter of a home match against Huddersfield Town, which the Rams were expected to win comfortably.

- SHEFFIELD U: Hope, Badger, Hemsley, Mackenzie, Colquhoun, Salmons, Woodward, Scullion, Dearden, Holmes, Ford.
- DERBY COUNTY: Boulton, Webster, Robson, Durban, McFarland, Todd, McGovern, Gemmill, O'Hare, Hector, Hinton.
- RESULT: Sheffield United 0, Derby County 4 (Gemmill 12, Durban 18, Hector 65, O'Hare 74).
- REFEREE: J. Taylor. • ATTENDANCE: 38,212. • POSITION: 1st.

Saturday 15 April

Derby County v Huddersfield Town

The comfortable 4-0 victory at Bramall Lane was exactly what was needed after two games without a win. The question now was could Derby see-off relegation threatened Huddersfield Town at the Baseball Ground? The Terriers had pulled off one of the biggest surprises of the season when the beat the Rams at Leeds Road at the end of November. Surely Derby wouldn't make the same mistake this time. With no injury worries Clough stuck to the same eleven that had been far too good for the Blades. Huddersfield Town included Trevor Cherry, later to play for Leeds, in their side along with the flamboyant Frank Worthington. The front page of *The Ram* carried an article promising that the club would not waste a penny of the £300,000 they were expecting from season ticket sales. Inside was a feature on Kevin Hector who had been back to his best form over the last few weeks under the headline 'King Kev at his greatest'.

Straight from the kick-off it was obvious that Clough's men were not going to underestimate their opponents the way they had in November. They were quickly on the attack and McFarland, with his head still bandaged after that nasty collision against the Magpies on Easter Monday, powered in a header that was well saved by 'keeper Pierce. On the quarter-of-an-hour mark the Rams were awarded a corner on the left and Hinton curled over a near-perfect cross and this time Pierce was well beaten by McFarland's powerful header. An early lead was exactly what the nervous Derby fans had wanted and seven minutes later they had more to shout about when Hector made it 2-0 after McGovern's shot had been deflected into his path by a Huddersfield defender. It was his 200th League goal overall.

A one-sided affair remained 2-0 at the interval but seven minutes after the resumption Hector crossed from the right beyond Lawson's near post and in came O'Hare to place a delicate header which had the 'keeper scrambling across his line but he was unable to prevent the ball from edging in at the far post.

After that the game began to fizzle out. There was no way back for the Terriers who had never mounted a serious attack and the Rams cruised to the 3-0 victory. Afterwards Clough described his side's performance as a very ordinary one. 'In fact we were rubbish,' he added. Obviously only the highest standards were going to satisfy the manager but his judgement did seem rather harsh.

Title contenders Leeds United were involved in an FA Cup semi-final with Birmingham City the same afternoon and Manchester City, who had won the previous two matches, could only draw at Coventry. Liverpool won 2-0 away at West Ham and were still very much in contention themselves. Derby now had two matches left. The next one would be at Manchester City's Maine Road the following Saturday and nine days after that Liverpool would be travelling to the Baseball Ground for the Rams' final game of the season. No wonder everyone was biting their finger nails.

- **DERBY COUNTY:** Boulton, Webster, Robson, Durban, McFarland, Todd, McGovern, Gemmill, O'Hare, Hector, Hinton.
- **HUDDERSFIELD T:** Lawson D., Clarke, Hutt, Smith S., Ellam, Cherry, Hoy, Dolan, Worthington, Lawson J., Chapman.
- **RESULT:** Derby County 3 (McFarland 15, Hector 22, O'Hare 52), Huddersfield Town 0.
- **REFEREE:** J. Yates. • **ATTENDANCE:** 31,414. • **POSITION:** 1st.

Saturday 22 April

Manchester City v Derby County

Although Leeds, Derby and Liverpool were all still very much in the running for the First Division title, Manchester City had begun to fade after being favourites a few weeks earlier. It was about that time that manager Joe Mercer decided to splash out £200,000 on the brilliant, if inconsistent, Rodney Marsh from QPR to add extra depth and flair to their talented squad.

City had been four points clear at the beginning of the month but although they narrowly overcame Chelsea on the day that Marsh made his debut, a single point from the next three games saw them back with the chasing pack. Disturbingly for the Maine Road faithful, it was being rumoured that his presence was still disrupting the squad.

Derby were unchanged from the side that had beaten Huddersfield but back in goal for second-placed City came goalkeeper Joe Corrigan who had missed seven games through injury and with centre-forward Wyn Davies out injured, Mike Summerbee was handed his number nine shirt with Francis Lee switching to the right wing.

At a packed Maine Road the home side were quickly out of the blocks. Marsh, seemingly determined to correct the impression that he had been responsible for the poor results since his arrival, was in sparkling form. A goal looked likely at any time when it came in the 26th minute it was Marsh himself on the mark after a superb run through the Derby defence ended with a cross shot past Boulton into the far corner. Even the huge contingent of Derby supporters on Moss Side had to concede that it was a particularly fine effort.

City could have added to the opener before the interval while Derby, despite the encouragement from the huge following, just couldn't get going. To make matters worse, four minutes before the interval Webster had to retire with a knee injury and was replaced by Hennessey. There would have to be a massive improvement if the Rams were to make a game of it in the second half.

Clough must have decided that Derby's best chance now lay in all-out attack and after the re-start his side began throwing

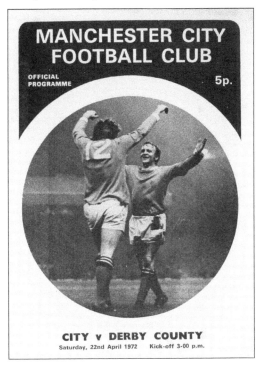

MANCHESTER CITY FOOTBALL CLUB

OFFICIAL PROGRAMME

5p.

CITY v DERBY COUNTY

Saturday, 22nd April 1972   Kick-off 3-00 p.m.

men forward in a frantic search for an equaliser and Hector went close. O'Hare twice grazed the woodwork and 'keeper Corrigan, who had been a spectator for most of the first half, was marking his return after injury with excellent saves from Robson and Hinton.

The second goal was always going to be vital and when it arrived in the 67th minute it was the home fans who were cheering. One again Marsh was instrumental. After evading Todd's challenge he raced into the penalty area where he was sent sprawling by Hennessey. Referee Burtenshaw had no alternative than to blow for a penalty and up stepped Lee to fire home his 15th successful spot-kick of the season. There was no way back for the Rams and City ran out deserved 2-0 winners.

Afterwards Clough said although the home team had been poor in the first half, Derby had been worse. 'Rodney Marsh isn't a bad player,' said the Derby manager before adding that he thought his side had no chance of winning the title now. As for the ebullient City assistant manager Malcolm Allison, he offered the opinion that Derby would still come top, adding, 'whoever does, it will be well-deserved because it is a very hard League'.

To make matters worse, Leeds won 1-0 at West Brom and Liverpool beat Ipswich 2-0 at Anfield so Derby had suddenly dropped down from first to third. It was obvious now that the last match of the season at home to Liverpool would be absolutely crucial. But even then the final outcome might not even be decided until the following Monday when Leeds and Liverpool were due to play away at Wolves and Arsenal respectively.

By then Clough's players would be out in sunny Majorca enjoying a well-deserved holiday. But if they could beat Liverpool, on the Monday they would be keeping a keen eye on results from Molyneux and Highbury.

- MANCHESTER CITY: Corrigan, Book, Donachie, Doyle, Booth, Jeffries, Lee, Bell, Summerbee, Marsh, Towers.
- DERBY COUNTY: Boulton, Webster, Robson, Durban, McFarland, Todd, McGovern, Gemmill, O'Hare, Hector, Hinton. Sub. Hennessey for Webster.
- RESULT: Manchester City 2 (Marsh 26, Lee 67 pen), Derby County 0.
- REFEREE: N. Burtenshaw. • ATTENDANCE: 55,023. • POSITION: 3rd.

April had been a mixed month for Derby. Although they had enjoyed well-deserved victories against Leeds and Sheffield United and had picked up another two points against lowly Huddersfield they had surprisingly come unstuck at home to Newcastle before losing the crucial match at Maine Road. On the bright side, McFarland who had suffered that nasty head injury against Newcastle, had been leading by example and Hector had come back to form at the right time.

As for centre-forward John O'Hare who had been magnificent all season, April was probably his best month of the lot and not just because of the crucial opener against Leeds on Easter Monday either. He had scored against Sheffield United and Huddersfield too and his general play had been exceptional. Surely even his biggest critics were convinced by now.

Although Manchester City were top of the table at the end of the month, they had completed their fixtures and were only one point ahead of second placed Liverpool who had two games left. Derby who were third on the same number of points as Liverpool but they had an inferior goal average. It was virtually impossible for City to clinch the title because the Rams and the Reds were still to play each other and both had a superior goal average. If Liverpool won at Derby in their last match of the season they would reach 58 points and overtake City and then it would depend on the Reds' final fixture away at Arsenal.

Leeds were also in with a good chance of finishing as champions. They had two games left and only needed a win to overtake City on goal average as long as they didn't lose the other match by a cricket score. Revie's men also had an FA Cup Final against Arsenal to contend with, so they were in with a chance of completing the double.

Top of the table at the end of April was as follows:

	P	W	D	L	F	A	Points
Manchester City	42	23	11	8	77	45	57
Liverpool	40	24	8	8	64	29	56
Derby County	41	23	10	8	68	33	56
Leeds United	40	23	9	8	70	29	55
Arsenal	39	21	7	11	57	38	49

May 1972

Champions at Last

Monday 1 May

Derby County v Liverpool

Just as we had been half expecting for weeks, the race for the Football League title was going to go right to the wire. Most pundits were of the opinion that either Leeds or Liverpool would emerge as champions with Derby rank outsiders.

Derby's last match of the season at home to Liverpool on Monday 1 May could go a long way to deciding the outcome because if Liverpool won they were bound to finish higher than the Rams and they still had the away fixture at Arsenal the following Monday. If Derby beat Liverpool it might depend on

the Ram

7p

Official Newspaper of Derby County F.C.

No. 30 (v. Liverpool, May 1, 1972)

League Championship Trophy

FIRST THE CENTRAL LEAGUE TITLE, THEN THE TEXACO CUP. . . CAN WE PULL OFF A HAT-TRICK WITH

The biggest prize of them all

BRIAN CLOUGH said it on BBC TV a week ago . . . the Football League Championship is the hardest prize of them all to win . . . the one which gives football people the most pleasure in taking.

Rams can lose the chance tosnight if they don't win. They must wait until next Monday if they beat Liverpool, even in the event that Leeds should fail tonight. 'Pool could still pull it off on goal average. What a finale.

COME OFF IT

STOP TRYING TO ROCK THE BOAT. THAT'S THE END-OF-SEASON ADVICE FROM DERBY COUNTY CHAIRMAN, MR. SAM LONGSON, TO THE *DERBY EVENING TELEGRAPH* AND ANYONE ELSE DISPOSED TO SNIPE AT THE CLUB.

'It's incredible that after the best season in the club's history we should be the subject of this sort of allegation', says the Chairman.

WHAT ALLEGA-TIONS? The sports edition of the local paper a fortnight ago ran a 'Why can't we concentrate on soccer?' story. It's a question we would ask them.

Especially the sports editor, who asked why Derby fans had to put up with rumours, still-continuing, that Manager Brian Clough and his assistant Peter Taylor, would be moving on to Coventry City. Suggesting that more money would satisfy the management he added: 'Brian Clough and Peter Taylor hardly need for me to ask for a rise on their behalf', giving the impression that salary problems were the basic reasons for the rumours. Stop the rumours, suggested the Telegraph, stoking the fires.

RUMOURS WILL ALWAYS ABOUND IN FOOTBALL, THEY ARE PART OF THE GAME. And top managers will always be the targets for ambitious clubs, no matter what.

Let's examine the other charges against the Derby County Board:

1 Mr. Clough is probably 'disappointed' that the Board have decided to shelve the building of a new stand for 12 months, so thwarting the club's potential. FACT: The Corporation have a demolition scheme which would clear a great deal of property around the Baseball Ground, making possible more expansion than now seems possible. 'We are waiting to see exactly what the position is because, as businessmen, we will not waste £300,000 to £400,000 now when the possibilities might be so much different very quickly', explains chairman Longson.

2 Rams signed the manager 'by chance' five years ago. FACT: It was not by chance that Mr. Longson and three directors went up to Scotch Corner to sign Mr. Clough and Mr. Taylor. The chairman had been checking

and asking questions for a long time. Nor was it by chance that same *Evening Telegraph* bitterly attacked the departure of previous manager, Tim Ward in May, 1967: "The Board of Directors are faced with a gigantic task to justify this clean sweep that will be the talk of Derby for a long time'.

3 Derby's wage bill is lower than all the top clubs, lower even than third from bottom Crystal Palace. FACT: This is rubbish. Rams employ fewer staff, fewer players . . . and this is, surely, a tribute to able management. 'It is impossible to refute this without revealing the salaries we pay, and this is confidential between us and our employees', says the Chairman, 'but I can say with confidence that our pay scales are in the top bracket'.

Mr. Longson pays tribute to the tremendous achievements

Turn to back page

FRESH FIGHT FOR RAMS

BEFORE THE Championship battle with Liverpool in front of an all-ticket Baseball Ground crowd, Derby County face another fight—to field a full-strength side.

Roy McFarland (groin) and Colin Todd (ankle) dropped out of the England squad for the West Germany game because of injuries, and Ron Webster was hurt in the defeat at Manchester City.

Rams need them badly against a side with 28 points from the last 30.

On top of everything else, Derby need one point—which would guarantee them third place—to 'qualify for Europe next season.

	P	W	D	L	F	A	Pts
Man. City	42	23	11	8	77	45	57
Liverpool	40	24	8	8	64	29	56
DERBY	41	23	10	8	68	33	56
Leeds	40	23	9	8	70	29	55

Colin Todd Rams' Player of the Year

A SALUTE to the Player of the Year, elected by the fans—and a narrow win for Colin Todd, who pipped skipper Roy McFarland in the voting after a record poll.

Third place went to Archie Gemmill, who moved above other Rams'

favourites thanks to a late surge in the voting (you needn't send us any more postcards now, Archie!).

'They're all Players of the Year'—see Page Two.

WELCOME TO LIVERPOOL FANS

how Leeds fared over their remaining two fixtures, one of which was at home to Chelsea that evening, followed by the away game at Wolves along with the outcome of Liverpool's match at Highbury in a week's time. Leeds also had that FA Cup Final against Arsenal to think about.

With Webster out of action following his unfortunate injury at Maine Road, Clough was expected to switch Todd to right-back as his replacement and bring in Hennessey who had come on as substitute at Maine Road. No wonder Derby fans were astonished when it was announced before the kick-off that 16-year-old Steve Powell would be playing instead. Otherwise the Rams were at full strength as were Liverpool's star-studded side.

As expected the Baseball Ground was full to capacity and there were also thousands of Liverpool fans in the streets surrounding the stadium unable to get in when referee Clive Thomas blew the whistle to get the game underway. The atmosphere inside the stadium was electric and it soon became obvious that the official was in no mood to let things get out of hand. Any sign of over-aggression on the pitch (always possible with the likes of Tommy Smith and Larry Lloyd around) was resulting in a free-kick.

Although Liverpool had gone unbeaten in the League since early January and had taken 28 points out of 30, they would probably be reasonably happy with a draw. Both points were essential as far as Derby were concerned and although they went close on a couple of occasions it remained scoreless at half-time. The tension had been affecting the players who were finding it impossible to play the sort of free-flowing football that had characterised their seasons.

Heighway and the dangerous duo of Keegan and Toshack were being well held by Derby's defence with McFarland and Todd in outstanding form. Young Powell, who was showing no signs of nerves, was having a superb game too and one brilliant piece of skill when he brought the ball down and flicked it over Emlyn Hughes' head before clearing to a colleague was quite exceptional.

Early in the second half it was becoming increasingly likely that one goal would be enough to settle it and Derby were beginning to look the more likely to break the deadlock. Seventeen minutes after the re-start Gemmill collected a Hector throw in before moving inside and passing to Durban who dummied, allowing the ball to reach McGovern, and the Scottish midfielder fired past 'keeper Clemence into the far corner. It was a magnificent goal.

Liverpool's best chance had fallen to Toshack after Keegan had beaten off Todd before whipping over a centre to his Welsh partner who failed to make the most of it. The Merseysiders' other chances fell to defenders Firstly Boulton was on his toes to save a long-range volley from Tommy Smith, Emlyn Hughes shot wide and then the 'keeper parried a powerful volley from Lawler. Manager Shankly brought on McLoughlin to replace Heighway and the Rams' 'keeper had to be on his toes again to save a shot from the substitute.

Durban was having a marvellous game in midfield. Hector and O'Hare were putting in fine performances too and it was Hector who came close to adding a second when Durban helped a McFarland header into his path but his shot skimmed off the crossbar after Clemence had managed to get his fingertips to it. With time running out, it was Durban in the thick of it again, this time in his own penalty area clearing up after a Liverpool raid. By now the tension had become almost unbearable with the Derby supporters urging referee Thomas to blow the final whistle and a couple of minutes into added time he obliged.

- DERBY COUNTY: Boulton, Powell, Robson, Durban, McFarland, Todd, McGovern, Gemmill, O'Hare, Hector, Hinton.
- LIVERPOOL: Clemence, Lawler, Lindsay, Smith, Lloyd, Hughes, Keegan, Hall, Heighway, Toshack, Callaghan. Sub. McLaughlin for Heighway.
- RESULT: Derby County 1 (McGovern 62), Liverpool 0.
- REFEREE: C. Thomas. • ATTENDANCE: 39,159. • POSITION: 1st.

Although Derby had won they were still outsiders for the title. Leeds had overcome Chelsea 2-0 at Elland Road on the same evening so it would all depend on the result of Liverpool's match at Arsenal and Leeds' game at Wolves, both of them scheduled for the following Monday evening. A win for Shankly's men would be enough for them to overtake Derby and Revie's side only needed a point to move above the Rams.

Thousands of Derby County fans were glued to their radio sets on the evening of Monday 8 May as reports of the two games trickled through. The last half hour seemed an eternity. Surely either Liverpool or Leeds would do enough to leapfrog the Rams but eventually the final whistles sounded. The best a frustrated Liverpool could muster was a scoreless draw while Leeds, with Revie trying everything in his power to secure the point required, had gone down 2-1 at Molyneux. Derby County, with their players holidaying in Majorca and their manager on holiday with his family on the Scilly Isles had won the coveted title for the first time in their history in just about the most dramatic way imaginable.

A few days later the squad and the management team of Clough and Taylor were back at the Baseball Ground being saluted by the massed ranks of euphoric supporters and thousands packed the streets of Derby when the victorious squad and the management team went on a tour of the town.

Some fans were still in a state of disbelief at what had happened. The whole thing was quite remarkable and Brian Clough, when interviewed on television, went even further describing winning the First Division title as one of the miracles of the twentieth century.

John McGovern scores the only goal of the game against Liverpool at the Baseball Ground on Monday 1 May. As it turned out a week later, it was enough to clinch the title for the Rams

The final League table of the season looked like this:

	P	W	D	L	F	A	Points
Derby County	42	24	10	8	69	33	58
Leeds United	42	24	9	9	73	31	57
Liverpool	42	24	9	9	64	30	57
Manchester City	42	23	11	8	77	45	57
Arsenal	42	22	8	12	58	40	52
Tottenham Hotspur	42	19	13	10	63	42	51
Chelsea	42	18	12	12	58	49	48
Manchester United	42	19	10	13	69	61	48
Wolves	42	18	11	13	65	57	47
Sheffield United	42	17	12	13	61	60	46
Newcastle United	42	15	11	16	49	52	41
Leicester City	42	13	13	16	41	46	39
Ipswich Town	42	11	16	15	39	53	38
West Ham U	42	12	12	18	47	51	36
Everton	42	9	18	15	37	48	36
West Brom A	42	12	11	19	42	54	35
Stoke City	42	10	15	17	39	56	35
Coventry City	42	9	15	18	44	67	33
Southampton	42	12	7	23	52	80	31
Crystal Palace	42	8	13	21	39	65	29
Nottingham F	42	8	9	25	47	81	25
Huddersfield Town	42	6	13	23	27	59	25

Up for the Cup

Although the quest for the First Division title was the priority for Derby County, almost as important was the FA Cup, which in some ways was more glamorous and often attracted bigger crowds. The Football League Cup wasn't far behind either and for the Rams that season there was the little matter of the Texaco Cup too, a sponsored tournament involving a total of 16 clubs from England, Scotland, Northern Ireland and the Republic.

The Football League Cup

Derby's all too brief journey in the Football League Cup began at the Second Round stage in August and their opponents were none other than their increasingly bitter rivals, Leeds United. The Rams' record in the competition since its inception in 1960 had been a modest one with the exception of the 1967-68 season, Clough's first at the Baseball Ground, when they reached the semi-final stage.

That season victories over Hartlepools, Birmingham, Lincoln and Darlington had propelled them to the semi finals and when the draw had been made supporters were greeted with the news that Leeds United would be their opponents. Unfortunately, Revie's side turned out to be far too strong for Derby. They won both legs before going on to beat Arsenal 1-0 in the final.

Now they were back again in the same competition, four seasons later, and likely to be equally formidable.

Wednesday 8 September

Derby County v Leeds United (Football League Cup 2nd Round)

Brian Clough fielded an extremely strong line-up for the tie with the emphasis on attack. The only change from the side that had won at Everton in the First Division on the Saturday was the return of O'Hare after injury with McGovern making way. Therefore, Wignall who had started the season well, would be partnering Hector and O'Hare up front. Don Revie included Harvey, Yorath, Belfitt and Madeley in his side with Sprake, Cooper, Jones and Gray taking a breather.

At a packed Baseball Ground Derby were soon mounting a series of attacks which prompted Revie to switch the versatile Madeley from the left wing to bolster his overworked defence. Hinton who was playing mainly on the right looked in prime form early on and Yorath was soon struggling to cope.

Durban came closest to opening the scoring after half an hour when he got his head to Gemmill's centre only for 'keeper Harvey to save with his feet. The match remained scoreless at half-time but shortly after the interval Hector went on a long run before passing to Hinton. His fierce shot seemed certain to break the deadlock but Charlton rescued the situation by clearing off the line with Harvey well beaten. When Leeds began to threaten, Clarke almost got on the score sheet only to slip at the vital moment.

Although the Rams had looked marginally the better side on the night and had been on the attack for long periods, both defences prevailed and a highly competitive match ended scoreless. Todd had put in another good performance keeping the dangerous Clarke quiet for the most part and Hunter was probably the pick of the determined Leeds defence.

One thing was certain; the replay at Elland Road at the end of the month would be another fierce encounter. Leeds would probably be more attack minded next time, which might give the Derby forwards slightly more space.

- **DERBY COUNTY:** Boulton, Webster, Robson, Todd, McFarland, Gemmill, Durban, Wignall, O'Hare, Hector, Hinton.
- **LEEDS UNITED:** Harvey, Reaney, Yorath, Bremner, Charlton, Hunter, Lorimer, Clarke, Belfitt, Giles, Madeley.
- **RESULT:** Derby County 0, Leeds United 0.
- **REFEREE:** • B Homewood. • **ATTENDANCE:** 34,023.

Monday 27 September

Leeds United v Derby County (Football League Cup 2nd Round replay)

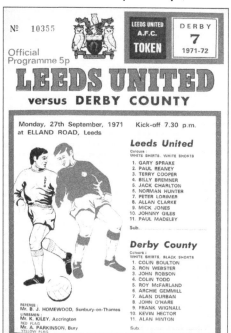

Nineteen days later Derby were off to Elland Road for the replay. The goalless draw at the Baseball Ground had been a bruising affair and another fierce battle was anticipated. Clough's side, which was still unbeaten after 11 games, included McGovern in place of the injured Durban. Back in the Leeds line-up were Sprake and Cooper with Harvey and Clarke making way,

Although the Rams in their new blue and yellow away strip started brightly, they were unable to beat 'keeper Sprake who saved well from Hector. Bremner then came off worst after a clash with Gemmill in the 25th minute and was replaced by Mann. Nine minutes later a Lorimer free-kick was blocked by the Derby defence. The ball eventually fell to full-back Reaney who nodded it back to Lorimer leaving the winger with the simple task of prodding a close range shot past Boulton to open the scoring.

Early in the second half Derby came within a whisker of equalising on three occasions with Gemmill, Hector and Robson all going close. A goal then might well have changed the outcome of the match but before long the Rams began to come under increasing pressure and a second goal for the home side was looking likely.

It duly arrived in the 63rd minute when McFarland brought down Madeley near the edge of the penalty area and the Derby wall was unable to prevent Lorimer firing powerfully past the 'keeper to make it 2-0. After that with Giles controlling the midfield there was no way back and the game ended with Leeds thoroughly deserving to go through to the next round.

- LEEDS UNITED: Sprake, Reaney, Cooper, Bremner, Charlton, Hunter, Lorimer, Yorath, Belfitt, Giles, Madeley. Sub: Mann for Bremner.
- DERBY COUNTY: Boulton, Webster, Robson, Todd, McFarland, Gemmill, McGovern, Wignall, O'Hare, Hector, Hinton.
- RESULT: Leeds United 2 (Lorimer 34, 63), Derby County 0.
- REFEREE: B. Homewood. • ATTENDANCE: 29,132.

The FA Cup

Derby County had enjoyed very little success in the FA Cup since the late 1940s and by now their one and only triumph in 1946 was but a distant memory. The nearest they had come to repeating their famous victory against Charlton had been in the 1947-48 season when they reached the semi-final stage before going out to Manchester United.

For around 30 years from the late 1940s only on rare occasions had they progressed beyond even the Third Round stage. The best they had mustered had been in the 1969-70 season when Clough's side reached the fifth round before going down 1-0 at QPR and the following year they lost at Everton at the same stage and with the same score line.

When the draw for the Third Round was made in December 1971, Derby were drawn at home to Third Division Shrewsbury Town so hopes were high that this might be the prelude to some long awaited success in the competition.

Saturday 15 January

Derby County v Shrewsbury Town (FA Cup 3rd Round)

As expected, Brian Clough fielded a full-strength line-up for the visit of Shrewsbury Town and although his side were soon mounting a series of attacks the visitors were quickly making clear that they weren't going to be a pushover. Hector was looking sharp but despite going close on a number of occasions the Rams were unable to break the deadlock and it remained scoreless at the interval.

After the resumption Shrewsbury continued to thwart the Rams forwards and although they conceded a series of corners they managed to hold firm until the 69th minute when Hector ran on to a clever through ball from McGovern and fired home off the underside of the crossbar.

After that the visitors began to buckle and when O'Hare got to a free-kick from Todd with five minutes remaining the ball ran loose to Hector who had ghosted into the danger area before shooting past 'keeper Mulhearn. Holton was booked for a foul on the lively Gemmill but although Derby continued to press up to the final whistle there were no further goals and they ran out comfortable 2-0 winners.

Afterwards Hector said he was delighted to see his goals go in, partly for himself but also because they were the culmination of a good team effort.

- DERBY COUNTY: Boulton, Webster, Robson, Durban, McFarland, Todd, McGovern, Gemmill, O'Hare, Hector, Hinton.
- SHREWSBURY T: Mulhearn, Brown, Fellows, Moore, Holton, Bridgwood, Roberts, Andrews, Wood, Moir, Groves.
- RESULT: Derby County 2 (Hector 69, 85), Shrewsbury Town 0.
- REFEREE: B. Homewood. • ATTENDANCE: 33,463.

CUP MATCH SPECIAL

the Ram

7p

Official Newspaper of Derby County F.C.

No. 20 (Saturday, February 5, 1972)

DERBY COUNTY

F.A. Cup   v.   Round 4

NOTTS COUNTY

BANNED

ENGLAND FORWARD Francis Lee, who has cracked 25 goals in Manchester City's rise to the top of the First Division, this week successfully appealed against the caution he got for a tackle on Colin Todd at the Baseball Ground in December, when the Rams won 3–1. Todd went specially to speak on Lee's behalf.

BUT, SAYS MANAGER BRIAN CLOUGH, THIS IS THE LAST OCCASION ON WHICH A DERBY COUNTY PLAYER WILL GIVE THIS KIND OF ASSISTANCE.

'We have always tried to play fair. When Colin was approached by Manchester City to support Lee, I told him to go if he wanted to and to tell the truth.

'The next morning, Frank O'Farrell was on the telephone. Why wouldn't we give evidence on behalf of Denis Law, who was cautioned here in the opening League game for failing to retire ten yards from a free-kick?

'I said no then, and because I don't wish the Club to be accused of inconsistency, everybody will get that answer from now on. I don't blame Frank for ringing, but it's his hard luck.

'THE HAND OF KINDNESS HAS NOT BEEN EXTENDED TO US VERY OFTEN TO RECIPROCATE FOR THE GESTURES WE MAKE. I DON'T SEE WHY WE SHOULD BAIL OUT ONE AFTER ANOTHER OF THE TEAMS WITH WHOM WE ARE CONTESTING THE CHAMPIONSHIP,' MR. CLOUGH TOLD US.

'Colin Todd now has three bookings after being cautioned last Saturday, including one for handling the ball. People are now getting away with similar offences.

'With Roy McFarland under a suspended sentence, we have enough problems of our own without going to bat for other clubs.

'WILL SOMEONE OFFER TO HELP GET OUR PLAYERS OFF? NOBODY HAS UP TO NOW.'

Is this our year?

The twin towers of Wembley are still a long way away but both Derby County skipper, England centre-half Roy McFarland (left) and Notts County captain Don Masson, signed from Middlesbrough a couple of years ago, have their eyes on the magic F.A. Cup.

Can Derby get to the F.A. Cup Final for the first time since their one and only Wembley win against Charlton in 1946? Or can Notts County become the first Third Division side to reach an F.A. Cup Final . . . and win promotion to Division Two as well?

We won't know the answers today. But, unless we get a draw, we'll know who goes into the bag for the Fifth Round draw, and the last 16, on Monday.

Saturday 5 February

Derby County v Notts County (FA Cup 4th Round)

Derby's opponents in Round 4 were Third Division Notts County. The front page of *The Ram* carried a headline posing the question Is This Our Year? Which might have been slightly premature.

The FA Cup was still extremely popular and it was unusual for the bigger clubs to field weakened sides against opposition from lower leagues. An all-ticket crowd of just under 40,000 packed the Baseball Ground including a huge contingent of Notts County supporters hoping for an upset. In fact the attendance was over 10,000 higher than that for the First Division match against Coventry the previous Saturday.

Derby fielded the same team that had beaten the Sky Blues and Notts County included ex-Rams favourite Willie Carlin in their line-up along with Tony Hateley and future international Don Masson.

It soon became clear that the Rams were going to be far too strong for their opponents who seemed overwhelmed by the occasion. Robson, who had scored Derby's winner a week earlier, put his side ahead in the 19th minute and the only surprise was that it took until a minute before the interval for them to double the lead through Hector.

Durban was having a field day and it was the midfielder who made it 3-0 early into the second half before adding another two minutes later. Hinton scored a fourth with a penalty but even then Derby weren't finished and when Durban completed a fine hat-trick to make it 6-0 there was still over a quarter of an hour to go. Young Steve Powell came on for O'Hare with eight minutes remaining but in the end a rampant Derby were content to play out time rather than inflict any more humiliation on their opponents although Notts, to their credit, had tried to play football rather than adopt a more robust approach.

- DERBY COUNTY: Boulton, Webster, Robson, Durban, McFarland, Todd, McGovern, Gemmill, O'Hare, Hector, Hinton. Sub: Powell for O'Hare.
- NOTTS COUNTY: Brown, Brindley, Worthington, Carlin, Stubbs, Jones, Nixon, Brad, Hateley, Masson, Cozens.
- RESULT: Derby County 6 (Robson 19, Hector 44, Durban, 56, 58, 74, Hinton 64 pen), Notts County 0.
- REFEREE: A. Morrisey. • ATTENDANCE: 39,450.

Saturday 26 February

Derby County v Arsenal (FA Cup 5th Round)

When the draw for Round 5 was made Derby supports were greeted with the good news that their side would be playing at home for the third time in the competition. On this occasion, though, they could expect a much sterner test because out of the hat for the Baseball Ground tie came FA Cup holders Arsenal.

The Gunners had not only lifted the coveted trophy the previous season, they were League Champions too and now they were coming into form after a hesi-tant start to the season. Although the Rams had won the First Division match between the two sides on home soil back in October, they had gone down 2-0 at Highbury only a fortnight ago.

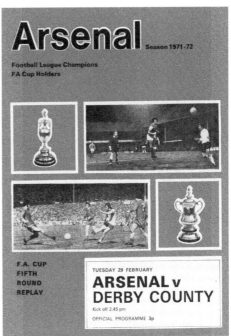

Both teams were at full strength with Derby unchanged for the sixth game in a row. Arsenal included Charlie George in their line-up along with England international midfielder Alan Ball who was at last beginning to make an impact after his transfer from Everton.

An all-ticket crowd of just under 40,000 which packed the Baseball

121

Ground included a large contingent of away supporters. George had scored both of his side's goals in the League match between the two sides and in a highly charged atmosphere it was the controversial striker who put the Gunners ahead just before the interval with a fine goal. Although the first half had been packed with action with both sides going flat out, the sheer tension of the occasion had prevented the sort of free-flowing football that everyone had been looking forward to.

Two minutes after the re-start Derby were awarded a penalty for a trip on O'Hare and Hinton beat 'keeper Bob Wilson from the spot to make it all square. After that it was anybody's game but Arsenal's more muscular approach was making it even more difficult for Derby to play their normal game.

With just 10 minutes remaining Charlie George put Arsenal ahead for the second time only for Durban to equalise with two minutes of normal time remaining after latching on to Hector's superb cross and placing the ball into the back of the net past 'keeper Bob Wilson. It was a dramatic end to an exciting, if at times over-physical, cup-tie.

The Gunners' 34 fouls to the Rams' 13 had reflected the difference between the two sides although only one player, George, had been booked after the referee Partridge, who had been particularly lenient up to then, decided he could not ignore his blatant trip on Gemmill.

The two sides would have to try again three days later at Highbury.

- DERBY COUNTY: Boulton, Webster, Robson, Durban, McFarland Todd, McGovern, Gemmill, O'Hare Hector Hinton.
- ARSENAL: Wilson, Rice, Nelson, Kelly, McLintock, Simpson, Armstrong, Ball, George, Kennedy, Graham. Sub: Storey for Kelly.
- RESULT: Derby County 2 (Hinton 47 pen, Durban 88), Arsenal 2 (George 41, 80).
- REFEREE: P. Partridge. • ATTENDANCE: 39,662.

Tuesday 29 February

Arsenal v Derby County (FA Cup 5th Round replay)

Over 63,000 were at Highbury for the replay with the gates closed 10 minutes before the kick-off. By then both sides knew that Leyton Orient would be the opponents in the next round so whoever the winners were they would fancy their chances of reaching the quarter-finals.

Storey was in the Arsenal line-up in place of Kelly but once again the Rams were unchanged. Although Derby were looking more skilful than their opponents in the first half they were unable to break down Arsenal's resolute defence. When the Gunners did push forward they found McFarland and Todd in magnificent form at the heart of the Rams' rear-guard. Ball and Kennedy did manage shots on goal eventually but Boulton was equal to the task.

At the other end Hinton floated over a couple of excellent crosses that beat 'keeper Bob Wilson but O'Hare was unable to convert the first after being badly obstructed and Gemmill's effort from the second was blocked.

Derby continued to dominate for long periods but were still unable to find a way to score the elusive goal that would almost certainly settle it. Arsenal brought on Radford to replace Kennedy and when the tie went into extra-time the Rams still looked the likelier of the two teams to force a result. In the end both had to settle for a second replay at Leicester City's Filbert Street ground in 13 days' time.

- ARSENAL: Wilson, Rice, Nelson, Storey, McLintock, Simpson, Armstrong, Ball, George, Kennedy, Graham. Sub. Radford for Kennedy.
- DERBY COUNTY: Boulton, Webster, Robson, Durban, McFarland Todd, McGovern, Gemmill, O'Hare Hector Hinton.
- RESULT: Arsenal 0, Derby County 0 (after extra time).
- REFEREE: P. Partridge. • ATTENDANCE: 63,077.

Monday 13 March

Arsenal v Derby County (FA Cup 5th Round second replay at Filbert Street)
Derby had not reached the sixth round of the competition since the 1949-50 season and if they were to get that far this time it would have to be the hard way. The two ties had been particularly gruelling affairs and this second replay coming just two days after a hard-fought win in the League at White Hart Lane was bound to be taxing.

Durban, who had missed the Spurs match, returned to the Rams side in place of Hennessey who was named as the substitute. As for Arsenal, their line-up was the same as the one that had held on to force the scoreless draw in the first replay.

The kick-off was delayed for 10 minutes to allow supporters from both sides who had been held up by heavy traffic to get in to the ground. Derby started brightly but the game was only four minutes old when McGovern attempted a back pass from all of 30-yards, which ricocheted off Todd into the path of Ray Kennedy who fired home past the advancing Boulton. It was a horrendous

error by the midfielder who should have played a simple pass upfield to Hinton instead and before long it was obvious that he was struggling to get over it.

Urged on by the tremendous support of around 20,000 fans, Derby were unable to find a way of breaking down the Gunners' defence on a hard playing surface. With 14 minutes remaining McGovern's miserable evening was complete when he picked up a nasty head injury after colliding with McFarland. The centre-half then pushed forward in a last ditch attempt to force an equaliser with Hennessey coming on to bolster the back four. It almost worked when McFarland put Hector clear but his low cross was scrambled away and soon afterwards the same player ran through on goal only to head narrowly wide from McFarland's cross. After that Arsenal held on grimly for their victory but for Derby it was back to League action and a home game with Leicester City five days later.

- DERBY COUNTY: Boulton, Webster, Robson, Durban, McFarland, Todd, McGovern, Gemmill, O'Hare, Hector, Hinton. Sub: Hennessey for McGovern.
- ARSENAL: Wilson, Rice, Nelson, Storey, McLintock, Simpson, Armstrong, Ball, George, Kennedy, Graham.
- RESULT: Arsenal 1 (Kennedy 4), Derby County 0.
- REFEREE: D. Smith. • ATTENDANCE: 40,000.

The Texaco Cup

Participation in the sponsored competition was by invitation with a total of 16 clubs taking part, six from England, six from Scotland, two from Northern Ireland and two from the Republic. The English sides were Manchester City, Stoke City, Coventry City, Huddersfield Town, Newcastle United and Derby. Scotland were represented by Falkirk, Hearts, Morton, Airdrieonians, Motherwell and Dundee United. Northern Ireland would supply Ballymena and Coleraine with Shamrock Rovers and Waterford representing from the Republic.

Brian Clough's attitude to his side's participation in the competition was that whatever its status might be, if you were in it you might as well try to win it, just as they had when they lifted the Watney Cup by beating Manchester United 4-1 in the final two seasons earlier so he decided early on to select his strongest possible sides, bearing in mind their First Division and FA Cup commitments.

Derby's opponents in the First Round were Scottish First Division side Dundee United.

Wednesday 15 September

Derby County v Dundee United (Texaco Cup 1st Round 1st leg)

Derby were without McFarland, Gemmill and Wignall all of whom were taking a break to allow minor injuries to clear up and into the side came Hennessey, McGovern and young Jeff Bourne on his first team debut.

In front of a crowd of just over 20,000 United wasted a couple of early chances but the Rams were soon on the attack and went ahead in the 12th minute when Durban headed home past 'keeper Mackay. Hinton then volleyed narrowly wide but shortly afterwards Hector rose to head the winger's cross to make it 2-0.

Walker came on at half-time in place of the injured Durban and a minute after the resumption the substitute scored Derby's third with his first kick of the ball. Three minutes later O'Hare placed a delicate header past the 'keeper to make it 4-0.

The visitors immediately pulled a goal back when Gordon's header caught Boulton out of position and seconds later the 'keeper was unable to get his hands to a miss-hit shot from Rolland and suddenly it was an unlikely 4-2. The Rams had lost their concentration and had paid for it with two sloppy goals.

Any thoughts that the Scottish side had about making a game of it evaporated in the 73rd minute when Hinton ran on to a clever flick from Hector to beat the advancing 'keeper. Even then Derby weren't finished and John Robson made it 6-2 nine minutes later with a long range shot that flew through a crowd of players into the back of the net. Derby's six goals had been scored by six different players and on this showing the second leg would be a formality.

- DERBY COUNTY: Boulton, Webster, Robson, Todd, Hennessey, McGovern, Bourne, Durban, O'Hare Hector, Hinton. Sub Walker for Durban.
- DUNDEE UNITED: Mackay, Gray, Cameron, Smith W., Smith D., Henry, Watson, Reid, Gordon, Rolland, Copland. Sub. Devlin for Copland.
- RESULT: Derby County 6 (Durban 12, Hector 25, Walker 46, O'Hare 49, Hinton 73, Robson 82), Dundee United 2 (Gordon 49, Rolland 50).
- REFEREE: G. Hartley. • ATTENDANCE: 20,059.

the Ram

Official Newspaper of Derby County F.C.

No. 6 (v. Dundee United, September 15, 1971)

All the INSIDE stories

INSIDE this issue—news of a Derby County record, a Brian Clough forecast that came true, John O'Hare at home, Tony Waddington on Derby County and Colin Todd. Always in THE RAM—latest team news, Roy McFarland and Brian Clough columns, Promotions news, Ram Pin-up (in colour). All the inside stories, for you and about YOU. Make sure you get your copy, on order from your local newsagent or from a Club seller before the kick-off. And now there are tokens, too.

GOALS galore in Dundee United's match on Saturday, when they visited rivals Dundee.
They scored four—but conceded six. United stars line up for *THE RAM.* Left to right—Back: Jim Cameron, Alex Reid, Alan Gordon, Hamish McAlpine, Donald Mackay, Walter Smith, Tommy Traynor, Billy Gray. Front: Andy Rolland, Denis Gillespie, Kenny Cameron, Joe Watson, Doug Smith, Jim Henry, Morris Stevenson, Davie Wilson.

The Ram   The Ram
DERBY COUNTY
2
Voucher

HELP US HELP YOU—POLICE

THE POLICE had a job on their hands before, during and after Saturday's local First Division 'derby' game against Stoke City—and once again came out of the fracas with great credit, writes DAVID MOORE.

Inspector Trevor Kitchener, supervising Pop-side control at the Baseball Ground, described some of the scenes as 'the worst I have seen in my 14 years' attendance at Derby County matches.'

There were three arrests before the game, two for being in possession of offensive weapons and the other for spraying paint from an aerosol can, and six inside the Ground (threatening behaviour, and assaults on the Police). Several spectators were ejected, and one youth was taken to Derbyshire Royal Infirmary with head injuries following a fall.

'Obviously, the fact that this was a 'derby' match heightened tension,' commented Chief Superintendent Harry Shelley afterwards.

And he issued this appeal to all regular supporters through *THE RAM:* 'Please keep well away from any trouble spots, even if it means waiting behind a few minutes for the Ground to clear. Some spectators do this, and it makes our job much more easy.

'If you become involved in a melee, however accidentally, it is possible that you may be jostled by Police when they take action. Should this happen, please accept our apologies in advance.

'I have known bystanders be knocked down, fortunately without injury, during a struggle. The only answer, as I say—*KEEP WELL CLEAR.*'

THREE BACK FOR RAMS

THREE changes by Derby County for tonight's Texaco Cup first-round first-leg game at home to Dundee United (7.30), plus one positional switch.

Roy McFarland (ankle), Archie Gemmill (thigh) and Frank Wignall (back), the latter pair having been nursing injuries, are out, and John McGovern and Jeff Bourne—he wears the No. 7 shirt, as he did in a couple of games last season—come in.

Alan Durban switches to inside right, and Jim Walker is substitute.

'We very much want to win this competition, and the changes definitely do not reflect a lack of interest,' says Brian Clough, Manager of the Rams. 'I'm likely to bring in Terry at any time, because he's as good a defender as we have got, while John McGovern is even better than Gemmill or Durban at marking up and winning the ball.'

Team: Boulton; Webster, Robson; Todd, Hennessey, McGovern; Bourne, Durban, O'Hare, Hector, Hinton. Sub.: Walker.

OFFICIAL NEWSPAPER AND PROGRAMME

127

Wednesday 29 September

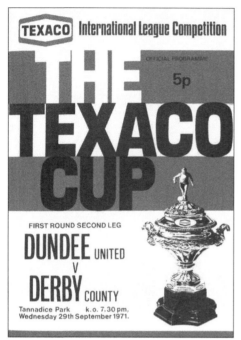

Dundee United v Derby County (Texaco Cup 1st Round 2nd leg)

Two weeks later Derby were in action at Dundee for the second leg. With three games in four days and a four-goal lead from the first leg, Clough opted to give Webster, Todd, O'Hare and Hector a well-deserved breather. Into the side came Daniel, Walker and Hennessey who had missed the last four League games along with young striker Barry Butlin and defender Tony Bailey on his debut.

Barring disasters, Derby were assured of a place in the next round. Hinton put them ahead in the third minute with a powerful shot after being set up by Gemmill and a quarter of an hour later Butlin tapped in a cross from Hinton to make it 2-0 on the night and an almost embarrassing 8-2 on aggregate.

After that the Rams began to take it easy and paid the price five minutes before the interval when Copland headed a corner past Boulton. Some slipshod defending allowed Devlin to equalise for the Tannadice outfit 15 minutes after the restart and with the Rams' defence looking totally out-of-sorts, Copland scored his second to make it a thoroughly disappointing 3-2 on the night.

Afterwards an annoyed Clough said, 'I never want to see a Derby side lose so sloppily again'. Also through were Coventry, Newcastle, Huddersfield and Stoke along with Airdrie, Shamrock Rovers and Ballymena and when the draw was made, Derby were up against old rivals Stoke in Round Two.

- DUNDEE UNITED: McAlpine, Rolland, Cameron, Markland, Gray, Henry, Trayner, Reid, Copland, Devlin, White. Sub: Smith for Devlin.
- DERBY COUNTY: Boulton, Daniel, Robson, Hennessey, Bailey, Gemmill, McGovern, Wignall, Butlin, Walker, Hinton.
- RESULT: Dundee United 3 (Copland 40, 67, Devlin 60), Derby County 2 (Hinton 3, Butlin 18). Derby won 8-5 on aggregate.
- REFEREE: E. Thomson. • ATTENDANCE: 6,000.

Wednesday 20 October

Derby County v Stoke City (Texaco Cup 2nd Round 1st leg)

Four days after suffering their first League defeat of the season at Old Trafford Clough decided to ring the changes for the Texaco Cup tie at home to Stoke City. Derby's reserve side had been doing well and this was an opportunity to give some promising young players a chance to shine at a higher level. It would also allow four first team regulars to have a rest. So in came left-back Alan Lewis and Steve Powell for their first team debuts. Powell at 16 years and 30 days was the club's youngest debutant beating the record of his father Tommy. Daniel and Wignall were also in the line-up with Robson, Durban, McGovern, and the injured Webster making way. Stoke's side included England 'keeper Gordon Banks and the ex-Manchester United forward, Jimmy Greenhoff.

On a sodden playing surface after heavy rain, Derby were soon dominating proceedings with young Powell showing what a fine prospect he was. His positional play and tackling were particularly impressive and he was quickly finding his teammates with some accurate passes. Lewis was also impressing the crowd of over 21,000, which was an excellent turnout under the circumstances.

O'Hare opened the scoring in the 10th minute, firing home from a narrow angle after rounding Banks and then made it 2-0 shortly before the interval when the England 'keeper could only parry a Wignall header. Stoke's Jackson replaced Jump at half-time and 10 minutes after the resumption Hector was on hand to fire home a left foot volley to increase Derby's lead. Bailey came on in the 66th minute after the unlucky Hennessey had picked up a knee injury but shortly afterwards Mahoney reduced the arrears for the visitors only for Greenhoff to make it an unlikely 3-2 in injury time.

It was a disappointing end to the match but at least it would make the second leg a more competitive affair.

- DERBY COUNTY: Boulton, Daniel, Lewis, Hennessey, McFarland, Todd, Wignall, Powell, O'Hare, Hector, Hinton. Sub: Bailey for Hennessey.
- STOKE CITY: Banks, Marsh, Pejic, Bernard, Smith, Bloor, Mahoney, Stevenson, Greenhoff, Jump, Haselgrave. Sub: Jackson for Jump at half-time.
- RESULT: Derby County 3 (O'Hare 10, 38, Hector 55), Stoke City 2 (Mahoney 64, Smith 87).
- REFEREE: N. Burtenshaw. • ATTENDANCE: 21,487.

Wednesday 3 November

Stoke City v Derby County (Texaco Cup 2nd Round 2nd Leg)

Two weeks later Derby travelled to Stoke's Victoria Ground for the second leg. With the final outcome so uncertain after Stoke's late comeback at the

Baseball Ground, Clough opted for a far stronger line-up than the one that had conceded the two unexpected late goals.

A large crowd were there to see the match and Texaco must have been delighted because attendances generally in the competition were remarkably high and it was getting plenty of attention in the media.

Although both sides went close in the first-half the game remained goalless at the interval. Fifteen minutes after the resumption Derby took the lead through Wignall whose deflected shot looped over the stranded Banks into the back of the net. With time running out it looked as though the goal would be enough to secure victory but with just four minutes remaining centre-half Denis Smith fired past Boulton from the edge of the area to equalise.

It was a case of too little too late for the Potters and Derby went through to the semi-final stage 4-3 on aggregate. Their opponents would be Newcastle United who had been far too good for Coventry with Airdrieonians taking on Ballymena in the other semi-final.

- STOKE CITY: Banks, Marsh, Pejic, Bernard, Smith, Bloor, Haslegrave, Mahoney, Conroy, Eastham, Jump. Sub: Stevenson for Eastham.
- DERBY COUNTY: Boulton, Webster, Robson, Todd, Hennessey, McGovern, Durban, Wignall, O'Hare, Hector, Hinton.
  RESULT: Stoke City 1 (Smith 86), Derby County 1 (Wignall 60). Derby County won 4-3 on aggregate.
- REFEREE: J. Hunting. • ATTENDANCE: 23,461.

Wednesday 24 November

Derby County v Newcastle United (Texaco Cup Semi-Final 1st leg)

Derby were unchanged from the team that had beaten Sheffield United at Bramall Lane in the First Division for the first leg of the Texaco Cup semi-final against Newcastle United who also fielded a strong line-up which included centre-forward Malcolm Macdonald.

In front of a crowd of just over 20,000 Derby went ahead in the 7th minute through O'Hare who collected a pass from Gemmill before shooting past 'keeper McFaul from the edge of the area. It remained 1-0 at the interval although Derby had looked the more convincing of the two sides. The only Newcastle threat had come from Macdonald who would need watching in the second half. Later, inside-forward Tony Green, Newcastle's expensive signing from Blackpool, was replaced by Tommy Gibb after feeling unwell and McFarland was booked along with Burton and Howard for the visitors.

The Rams should have made the second leg a formality after continuing to dominate but in the end had to settle for the narrow victory. Afterwards Joe

Harvey, the Newcastle manager, announced that he was quite satisfied with the result and reckoned his side had a fair chance of progressing to the final in front of what he thought would be a crowd of over 30,000 at St James' Park.

- DERBY COUNTY: Boulton, Webster, Robson, Todd, McFarland, Hennessey, McGovern, Gemmill, O'Hare Hector, Hinton.
- NEWCASTLE U: McFaul, Craig, Clark, Howard, Burton, Nattrass, Barrowclough, Green, Macdonald, Tudor, Hibbitt. Sub: Gibb for Green.
- RESULT: Derby County 1 (O'Hare 7), Newcastle United 0.
- REFEREE: C Thomas. • ATTENDANCE: 20,021.

Wednesday 8 December

Newcastle United v Derby County (Texaco Cup Semi-Final 2nd leg)

Two weeks later Derby travelled to Newcastle for the second leg. Clough decided to give a first start to the promising Tony Bailey who had already made one appearance as a substitute in the competition and had been play-

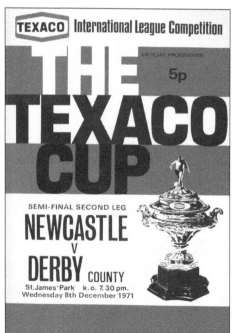

ing well in the successful reserve side. Daniel and Hennessey were also in the team allowing Robson, McFarland and Gemmill to take a break. Todd switched to right-back with Webster in an unaccustomed left-back slot,

In front of a crowd over 37,000 Bailey was booked in the first minute for clattering into Malcolm Macdonald. Any thoughts that Derby could rely on their one goal advantage from the first leg vanished when the home side went 2-0 in front through goals either side of half-time from the excellent

Macdonald and winger Barrowclough. The Rams recovered their composure later in the second half and Walker, who had come on for Hinton, made it 2-1 on the night and 2-2 on aggregate with a well-taken goal in the 73rd minute after collecting Durban's excellent centre and beating 'keeper McFaul.

Neither side would have wanted another 30 minutes but 12 minutes into extra-time McGovern scored for Derby direct from a corner and six minutes later Todd capped a fine come-back with a goal to see his side through to the final.

Derby supporters had enjoyed the competition so far and had turned up in numbers to watch the games. Now they could look forward to the two-leg final where their opponents would be Airdrieonians who had beaten Ballymena 7-3 on aggregate. The first leg was scheduled for Wednesday 26 January at Airdrie's Broomfield Park

- NEWCASTLE U: McFaul, Craig, Clark, Nattrass, Burton, Howard, Barrowclough, Green, Macdonald, Hibbitt, Coulson. Sub: Gibb for Coulson.
- DERBY COUNTY: Boulton, Todd, Webster, Hennessey, Bailey, Daniel, Durban, McGovern. O'Hare, Hector, Hinton. Sub: Walker for Hinton.
- RESULT: Newcastle United 2 (Macdonald 44, Barrowclough 60), Derby County 3 (Walker 73, McGovern 102, Todd 108).
- REFEREE: F. Nicholson. • ATTENDANCE: 37,140.

Wednesday 26 January

Airdrieonians v Derby County (Texaco Cup Final, 1st leg)

Four days after an exciting 3-3 draw away at West Ham in the First Division Derby were travelling north of the border to take on Scottish side Airdrieonians in the first leg of the Texaco Cup Final. Clough selected a side containing six first team regulars plus Hennessey with McFarland, Durban, McGovern, O'Hare and Hector saved from travelling.

There had been tremendous interest in the match locally and a crowd of 16,000 packed into Airdrie's compact Broomfield Park Ground to see what turned out to be a physical encounter. The home side, who were bottom of

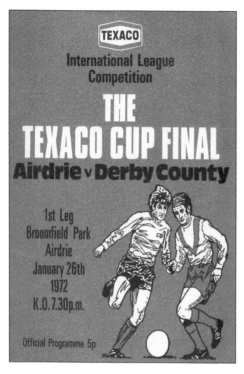

the Scottish First Division, did the bulk of the attacking but they were unable to break down the Rams' defence which included Tony Parry on his debut.

With Butlin, Davies and even Hector struggling to make an impact up front and wide-men Hinton and Walker unable to find their best form, the game ended scoreless. The destiny of the trophy would now depend on the second leg due to take place at the Baseball Ground on 8 March. As it turned out, it would be another seven weeks after that before the two sides locked horns again.

- AIRDRIEONIANS: McKenzie, Jonquin, Clarke, Menzies, McKinlay, Whiteford D., Wilson, Walker, Busby, Jarvie, Cowan. Sub: Whiteford J for Cowan.
- DERBY COUNTY: Boulton, Webster, Robson, Todd, Daniel, Hennessey, Parry, Gemmill, Butlin, Walker, Hinton.
- RESULT: Airdrieonians 0, Derby County 0. • ATTENDANCE: 16,000.

Wednesday 26 April

Derby County v Airdrieonians (Texaco Cup Final 2nd Leg)

A crowd of just over 25,000 were in the Baseball Ground for the 7.30pm kick-off for the second leg of the Texaco Cup Final. It was a remarkable attendance by any standards although by then thoughts were already turning to the crucial First Division match against Liverpool the following Monday.

Exhausted and disappointed after the defeat the previous Saturday to title rivals Manchester City, Clough decided to make changes, which wasn't altogether surprising considering that, arguably, the most important match in the club's history was only five days away.

Webster who had been injured at Maine Road was unfit and would probably miss the Liverpool match too. McFarland made way for the reliable Daniel at centre-half, Powell came in for Webster, Hennessey and Butlin replaced Todd and Gemmill and making his debut at centre-forward in place of O'Hare was Roger Davies who had been banging in the goals for the reserves

Derby had been largely content to stay on the defensive and contain the Airdrie attack in the first leg at Broomfield Road in January. It had been a bruising affair but this time the Rams were well on top throughout most of the first half although finding a way of breaking down the stubborn visitors' defence was proving more difficult than expected.

McKinley and Derby debutant Davies were booked after tangling as the match started to became even more competitive. It wasn't until the 40th minute that the Rams finally found a way through. The elusive Hector was pulled down in the box by 'keeper Roddy Mackenzie and Hinton made no mistake from the spot to open the scoring.

Six minutes after the interval Davies headed Derby's second from Butlin's cross only for the visitors to pull a goal back through Whitehead with around 12 minutes of normal time remaining. Although the Rams had a couple of nervy moments later they held firm for a deserved 2-1 victory in what had been another extremely physical match.

Durban, skipper for the night, received the Texaco trophy from Football League President Len Shipman before the players went on a deserved lap of honour, which unfortunately had to be curtailed when some over-enthusiastic supporters decided to join in.

- DERBY COUNTY: Boulton, Powell, Robson, Durban, Daniel, Hennessey, McGovern, Butlin, Davies, Hector, Hinton.
- AIRDRIEONIANS: Mackenzie, Caldwell, Clarke, Menzies, McKinley, Whiteford D., Wilson, Walker, Busby, Jarvie, Cowan. Sub: Jonquin for Cowan.
- RESULT: Derby County 2 (Hinton 40 pen, Davies 51), Airdrieonians 1 (Whiteford 78)
- REFEREE: J Taylor. • ATTENDANCE: 25,102.

It had been a most enjoyable competition. Boulton, Hennessey and Hinton played in all eight games, Hector, McGovern, Robson and Todd turned out six times and O'Hare five. It also presented an opportunity to see how younger players and fringe members of the squad were progressing. Derby County not only won the competition but promising young players such as Roger Davies, Jeff Bourne, Barry Butlin, Alan Lewis and Tony Bailey had been given their chance to shine.

In Reserve

Derby County reserves had an outstanding season. The team, managed by John Sheridan, not only won the Central League, they began to develop some promising young players. A few of them were also involved in the Texaco Cup and by the end of the season a handful looked capable of eventually playing regularly in the first team.

The Central League consisted of the reserve sides of First and Second Division clubs from the north of England and parts of the Midlands and Derby's season got off to an inauspicious start with a 1-0 defeat away to Manchester United. With Old Trafford closed because of crowd trouble in a match against Newcastle the previous February the fixture was switched to Macclesfield. Derby had most of the possession but a lack of punch in front of goal cost them dear. Young Steve Powell in midfield had a fine match and 16-year-old 'keeper Turner also did well.

Lack of firepower continued to hamper the side and they made it three defeats in a row, going down 4-0 at Coventry and then losing 2-0 at home to Stoke. Durban had played in the Coventry match but Derby's best player was Walker. Four days later a goal from Barry Butlin was enough to overcome Blackpool and the following Saturday they won 3-0 at Preston with Jeff Bourne getting a hat-trick. Butlin was on the mark in the next match with Derby's goal in a 1-1 draw at home to Blackburn. Catching the eye that day in Rovers' side was goalkeeper Graham Moseley and a few weeks later he was transferred to Derby. The following Saturday Ricky Marlow grabbed a brace in a 3-3 draw at home to Burnley.

Terry Hennessey was in the side for a 0-0 stalemate at Bolton and a few days later Roger Davies, who had recently been signed from Worcester City, scored a last minute winner against West Brom on his debut. It was a perfect way for the tall striker to kick-off his career with the Rams. Clough had paid £14,000 for him, which was a record fee for a non-League player. A 2-0 defeat at Hillsborough the following Tuesday was disappointing and four days later they were no match for a strong Everton who won 3-1.

The last two games apart, September had been a splendid month for Sheridan's side which by now was a well-balanced combination of youth and experience. They had shot up the Central League table and the following Saturday a crowd of over 8,000 were at the Baseball Ground to see them take on Manchester United. Making his debut was Moseley but although the new 'keeper impressed it was Butlin who made the news scoring both goals in the 2-0 victory against a United side that included Paddy Crerand, Ian Ure and Jimmy McIlroy. By now it was beginning to look as though Derby had a clutch of promising young players on their books.

A 1-0 win away at Newcastle was followed by a particularly encouraging performance in the 3-1 victory at home to Sheffield Wednesday and after overcoming Bury the month of October ended with a hard-fought 1-1 draw against an experienced Forest side with Butlin on the mark again. A 2-0 away win at Villa Park was Derby's sixth game without defeat and they continued their march towards the top of the table the following Saturday by winning 2-0 at home to Wolves with Davies and Bourne on the score sheet.

Two late goals by Sheffield United in late November after Walker had put Derby ahead were enough to inflict a rare defeat but with Davies in outstanding form, a 4-1 victory at home to Huddersfield took the Rams reserves up to third place.

With the halfway mark approaching they were mounting a strong challenge for honours. Everton were top after 19 matches with Bolton second and Derby third. By now young striker Roger Davies was looking increasingly lively and there had been some good performances from Peter Daniel, Steve Powell and Alan Lewis. Tony Bailey, who was a regular in the side, had been playing well too. Strikers Jeff Bourne and Barry Butlin were also catching the eye and left winger Jim Walker was showing why he was a more than adequate replacement if ever Hinton was out of action.

A 3-3 draw at Maine Road at the beginning of December was followed by a thrilling fight back against a star-studded Liverpool at the Baseball Ground. Bourne had given Derby the lead but two Liverpool goals including one from Toshack seemed to have secured victory only for Bourne to equalise in the 78th minute and with only six minutes remaining John Sims hit the winner.

After a fighting performance in a 2-1 win at Stoke a week before Christmas another large crowd of over 6,000 were at the Baseball Ground at the end of December to see Derby reserves take on a Leeds United side that included Terry Yorath, Eddie Gray and Joe Jordan. Colin Todd, who was recovering from injury, was in a strong line-up, which also included Alan Durban. A late penalty converted by Bourne after Davies had been felled was enough to secure a 1-0 victory a day after Derby's first team had been outplayed at Elland Road, losing 3-0.

By now Derby's reserve side had moved into second place behind leaders Everton after 24 games. They had been turning in some extremely impressive performances, which prompted a delighted John Sheridan to say that he thought his side would hold its own in the Fourth Division.

An outstanding display in a 3-0 win at Burnley on New Year's Day kept Derby second, five points behind Everton who were running out of steam although there was concern that Sheridan's side were beginning to be hampered by a series of postponements. A Roger Davies goal four minutes before the end at Blackpool looked as though it would be enough to guarantee a 15th win but a late equaliser from the home side meant they had to settle for a point. But with only Everton of the top six winning, Derby remained in second place, seven points adrift now, but with two games in hand.

Reserve team fixtures were still being disrupted by the weather although Derby came away from Nottingham Forest's City Ground on Saturday 19 February with a 5-3 victory on a day when none of their rivals won. It was a particularly rusty Derby defence that had conceded the three goals. A week later, missed chances at home to Aston Villa with Butlin and Bourne the main culprits meant that Derby had to be content with a goalless draw but at least the defence had been much tighter.

Now they were just four points behind leaders Everton with two games in hand. Butlin and Bourne were leading scorers with 14 goals each and Roger Davies was showing why Clough had paid that record fee for a non-League player. He had notched up 10 already and his general play was improving all the time. 'keeper Moseley was impressing too and Powell was showing great promise.

A goal from Bourne and another top class display from Moseley helped Derby to a narrow 1-0 win away at Wolves in early March, which was followed by another victory on their travels, this time against an experienced West Brom side with Butlin grabbing the goal. Next came a crucial top-of-the-table clash with Everton at the Baseball Ground, which Derby won 3-1 with goals from Bourne (penalty), Sims and Butlin. This was followed by a 5-1 trouncing of lowly Bury on the following Monday afternoon.

March had been a splendid month. Although they struggled to beat Newcastle 2-1, Derby had moved to within a point of the Merseysiders and with three games in hand were looking odds-on for the title. A goalless draw against defence-minded Sheffield United might have been a disappointing affair but they were back on the winning trail a few days later on Monday 10 April with a 6-1 thumping of Bolton Wanderers in a re-arranged match at the Baseball Ground in which injury-hit Hennessey had a run-out.

By now the side was going from strength to strength. A 2-0 win at Huddersfield was the prelude to two convincing home wins, the 5-0 against Preston followed by a 4-0 victory over Manchester City.

Unbeaten in 20 games, confidence was sky-high when Derby took on Coventry City for their final home match of the season at the end of April.

The visitors went ahead early on through Green but with Derby looking the better side Butlin hooked in a deserved equaliser in the 20th minute. A penalty from Bourne and another goal from Butlin, this time from a rebound after Davies had seen his shot come back off the crossbar, put Derby 3-1 ahead and Davies volleyed home a fourth after 62 minutes. Although Coventry hit back with two late goals from Green to complete his hat-trick, Derby held on for the 4-3 victory to clinch the title in front of a crowd of 5,300.

Although Everton had completed their fixtures, Derby had two games left. The first, away at Liverpool, ended goalless and in the last match of the season at Elland Road an 'experimental' side drew 1-1 which stretched their lead over Everton to three points. John Sheridan's side had gone unbeaten in 23 games going all the way back to December during which they had dropped just six points.

Keeper Moseley who won England Youth honours had never been on the losing side since his transfer from Blackburn in September. Strikers Jeff Bourne, Barry Butlin and particularly Roger Davies had impressed too. Their combined total of 63 goals had seen Derby finish up as the highest scorers with 84 goals, two more than Everton, and they had the best defensive record too.

Jim Walker had shown that he was still an extremely useful squad player and although Peter Daniel hadn't figured in the first team he had shown enough in the reserves to convince the manager he was worth persevering with. Tony Bailey had been superb all season and had deserved his first team opportunity at Christmas. It was unfortunate that it had come at Elland Road on a day when the whole side were way below their best. But arguably the most exciting prospect of all was 16-year-old Steve Powell. Injury permitting, the son of a Derby County legend seemed certain to have a fine future. The top of the table at the end of the season looked like this:

	P	W	D	L	F	A	Points
Derby County	42	26	10	6	84	39	62
Everton	42	25	9	8	82	41	59
West Brom	42	18	18	6	70	43	54
Liverpool	42	21	10	11	70	42	52

- APPEARANCES: Daniel 40, Bailey 40, Bourne 40, Butlin 35, Mason 32 (4), Walker 35, Stone 30 (2) Lewis 31, Powell 30 (1), Moseley 24, Davies 23, Turner 18, Parry 16, Sims 14 (2), Blair 11 (3), Marlowe 8 (3), Toon 7 (1), Hennessey 6, Durban 4, Phelan 1 (2), McFarland (1), Webster 1, Wignall 1, Todd 1, Thompson 1, Griffin 1, Sheridan 0 (1)
- SCORERS: Butlin 24, Bourne 23 (6 pens), Davies 16, Walker 9, Sims 3, Marlowe 2, Daniel 2, Toon 1, Parry 1, Mason 1, own-goals 2 (Mann, Man City, Serella, Forest).

A proud Brian Clough holds the Football League Championship trophy on the Council House balcony in front of his adoring fans.

Didn't They Do Well

Brian Clough's Derby County were often praised for their attractive style of football played mainly on the ground but their success was based largely on a fine defence and a strong spine. The manager maintained that football was a simple game and that it was a crime to give the ball away. There was nothing complicated about it and there was no need to over-elaborate. Every player understood what his job was and he was expected to do it, week in week out. As Clough, memorably, once said, 'That's what I pay you for'.

Ten of the squad played in 38 or more League matches and in most of the various cup-ties too. Achieving that was a tribute to their stamina and a willingness to turn out when less than 100 percent fit. It almost goes without saying that Clough and Taylor had generated a first class team spirit across the squad in which players respected each other's ability and efforts.

The Derby County squad at the beginning of the 1971-2 season
Back row: Jimmy Gordon (trainer), Peter Daniel, Kevin Hector, John McGovern,
Colin Boulton, Terry Hennessey, Frank Wignall, John Robson, Brian Clough (man-
ager). Front row: Peter Taylor (assistant manager), Alan Durban, John O'Hare,
Archie Gemmill, Roy McFarland, Alan Hinton, Colin Todd, Ron Webster.
Missing from the magnificent sixteen are Jim Walker, Steve Powell and Tony Bailey.

With McFarland and Todd away on England duty the rest of the Derby County squad
celebrate at the Baseball Ground in front of their jubilant supporters on the Sunday
morning after collecting their medals.

The backbone of Boulton, McFarland and O'Hare was one of the best in the country and all three were magnificent that season. Full-backs Webster and Robson were excellent too and the versatile Hennessey, although often restricted through injury, performed to a high standard in central defence or even in midfield when asked to do so.

There was no shortage of pace in the team with Todd, Gemmill and Hector outstanding in that department. Although Derby were renowned for their passing style with Durban and McGovern prominent, on the rare occasions when a more direct approach was necessary they were able to launch a long pass upfield to O'Hare who was a master at holding on to the ball and taking the pressure off the defence before finding a colleague with a pass. And of course there was winger Hinton whose crossing ability, shooting and mastery from the penalty spot were second to none.

Colin Boulton and Kevin Hector were ever-presents in the League and John Robson missed just one match. Todd, Gemmill and O'Hare were absent just twice and McGovern started on 39 occasions plus one more as a substitute. Webster, McFarland and Hinton played 38 League games and Alan Durban, whose place in the side seemed in doubt at the start of the season, finished up with 31 appearances. As for the unlucky Terry Hennessey, he managed 17 starts plus another as a substitute leaving Wignall as the only other player in double figures with those 11 appearances early in the season before being unexpectedly transferred to Mansfield in November. It was quite remarkable.

Not just that, virtually the same line-up represented Derby in the four pre-season matches as well as the seven League Cup and FA Cup games. Only in the Texaco Cup did Clough give some of his charges a breather which allowed him to assess the merits of a number of fringe players such as Peter Daniel, Tony Parry, Barry Butlin, Jeff Bourne and Alan Lewis along with the immensely promising new striker Roger Davies.

Colin Boulton

This was the season that it came good for Colin Boulton. After all those years playing second fiddle to Reg Matthews and then Les Green he had finally cemented his place in the side. If goalkeepers were judged purely on sheer consistency and reliability then Boulton was among the very best in the country.

Not particularly tall, at least by today's standards, he was probably at his peak that season and it is unlikely that Derby's 23 clean sheets in League matches could have been achieved without a 'keeper of his quality.

Boulton had a very safe pair of hands (after all, he was a good wicket-keeper too) and preferred to catch the ball cleanly rather than punch it away. Not one to come dashing off his line, he was also an excellent shot-stopper. His temperament was first class too. In fact just about the only time he did lose his temper was in the Texaco Cup final against an over-aggressive Airdrieonians side when he was probably fortunate to get away with a booking.

Although Clough always maintained that he was on the look-out for better players and was often linked with the brilliant young Peter Shilton, then at Leicester, Boulton later had the distinction of being the only Derby County player to play in all 84 matches of their two Championship winning seasons. So perhaps no one should have been surprised when in 2009, like six other members of the 1971-72 squad, he was selected in the Rams' best ever side above Shilton who, joined the club 16 years later.

Ron Webster

One of the features of the season was the consistently high performance of Belper born Ron Webster. His reliability had already become legendary at the Baseball Ground as had his sheer professionalism and it was a joy to supporters to see him become an integral part of a great side. Sadly for him, one of the four League matches he missed was the crucial encounter with Liverpool at the beginning of May after picking up an injury in the defeat at Manchester City's Maine Road ground nine days earlier. Fortunately young Steve Powell rose to the occasion.

Thanks to his excellent positional sense and firm tackling, wingers rarely got the better of him although for some reason he always seemed to have difficulty in containing Derek Wagstaffe, the Wolves wide-man. Webster may not have been blessed with great height but he was competent enough in the air and although wing-backs as such hadn't been 'invented', he could be effective when surging down the right flank. In fact, his fine headed goal in the 3-1 victory at home to Manchester City was a contender for goal of the season.

Webster had joined the Rams over a decade earlier in June 1960, making his debut on the right side of midfield towards the end of the 1961-62 season. He continued to perform superbly in that role for another six years and it wasn't until halfway through the 1967-68 season, Brian Clough's first at Derby, that he eventually switched to full-back, a position he continued to fill with distinction until he tried his luck in the USA in 1976. By then he had made 535 appearances for Derby in all competitions including five as a substitute, a total exceeded only by Kevin Hector.

John Robson

John Robson might have been one of Derby County's less well known players but no one who watched him regularly was in any doubt that the stylish left-back was an invaluable member of the squad. By now the player who had been picked out by Peter Taylor while playing junior football in the North-East was in his fourth season with the Rams but his sheer consistency more or less guaranteed his regular place in the team. So it came as no great surprise when his sharp tackling and an ability to overlap down the left-wing came to the attention of Sir Alf Ramsey who handed him a place in his England Under-23 side.

Robson would have been an ever-present but for an injury in the 3-1 win against Manchester City at the beginning of December which kept him out of the reckoning for the away fixture at Anfield a week later. Earlier, his brilliant goal against Nottingham Forest in the 2-0 victory at the City Ground had been rapturously received by supporters and at the end of January he was on the mark again, scoring the only goal of the game against Coventry.

Although Robson lost his place in Derby's side the following season following the acquisition of David Nish from Leicester, he went on to enjoy success with Aston Villa until, sadly, his career came to a premature end in 1978 after contracting multiple sclerosis. Tragically, he passed away in 2004 at the age of 53.

Roy McFarland

There was concern all round when it became apparent that Roy McFarland would not be able to play in Derby's opening fixture at home to Manchester United after it was revealed that he was still recovering from a nasty bout of influenza. It wasn't until the fourth match of the season that he finally made his first appearance and although it took him a couple of games to find his feet he soon began to recapture the sort of form that had thrilled supporters since his capture from Tranmere Rovers three years earlier. With the exception of Texaco Cup matches, for which Clough sometimes decided to give him a breather, his only other absence all season was in the 3-2 defeat at Anfield which was a game that the Liverpudlian, no doubt, would have relished.

By now the Rams' skipper was recognised by most observers as the best centre-half in English football and, barring injury, it seemed fairly certain that he would be an integral part of Sir Alf Ramsey's England set-up for the foreseeable future. Not only was he a formidable defender, strong in the tackle and excellent in the air, he was extremely dangerous in the opposition's penalty area too. His four goals that season were evidence that he could have been just as effective in a more attacking position and some were of the opinion that he could have played virtually anywhere.

Not only were his performances little short of majestic once he had returned to full fitness in September, he also captained the side superbly. Taking over the skipper's role from Dave Mackay would have been a daunting prospect for most men but McFarland proved he was more than capable of doing the job. Sadly, he was unable to receive the First Division trophy at a euphoric Baseball Ground from League President Len Shipman in May because he was on England duty.

Colin Todd

Colin Todd was absolutely magnificent throughout the season and was deservedly voted Player of the Year. In truth, the coveted award could have gone to almost any one of half a dozen players but few would argue that Todd reigned supreme.

It is extremely unusual for a defender to be thought of as exciting to watch but Todd was. His tackling was clinical, his pace electric, his positional sense first class and he could invariably find a man with a pass, long or short. He had a powerful shot too and both of his League goals were spectacular affairs. Rather like McFarland, who accepted the captaincy following Mackay's departure, Todd had been handed the unenviable task of wearing the Scottish international's number six shirt at the heart of Derby's defence. Some players might have been fazed by it, even if Mackay was coming to the end of his glorious career, but Todd rose to the challenge and quickly became a firm favourite with supporters.

By now his central defensive partnership with McFarland was the best in England and Todd was being compared to Bobby Moore with some pundits marking him out as Moore's natural successor for his country. When necessary, though, Todd could perform almost as well at full-back. So much so that when the England manager called him up for his first international appearance against Northern Ireland in the Home International Championship at the end of the season it was as a replacement for Paul Madeley at right-back. Later, of course, many of his 27 England caps were in central defence, often partnering his Derby teammate.

Alan Durban

Alan Durban's ninth season with Derby was another splendid one. Only a handful of players survived the Clough cull in the late 60s but it hadn't taken long for the new manager to appreciate what he had inherited and Durban went from strength to strength.

All the same, he may have been slightly unsure of his place in the side when the season began because Clough had opted for a two-man midfield. He was named as substitute in the first four League games before eventually making his first start in the home game against Southampton. But once the manager had decided to play three in midfield instead of relying on the pairing of McGovern and Gemmill, a regular place in the side was all but inevitable.

Durban had the ability to ghost through the opposition's defence and feed his colleagues with accurate, penetrating passes as well as nipping in with some important goals. If England's Martin Peters, was 10 years ahead of his time then Durban was probably in front of him.

His positional sense, intelligence and football brain made up for any lack of pace and he went on to prove what an important player he was, adding balance and subtlety along with those vital goals. Six in the First Division might have represented a modest return by his standards (he had been by a distance the club's leading goal scorer in the 1960s when playing further forward at inside-left) but he was more prolific in the FA Cup that season with four goals in five matches including a hat-trick in the 6-0 win over Notts County at the Baseball Ground.

John McGovern

If there had been an award that season for work rate, non-stop running and sheer enthusiasm then John McGovern would almost certainly have won it. His unselfish play, firm tackling and interceptions and a natural reluctance to give the ball away allowed Gemmill and Durban to play further forward in support of Hector and O'Hare.

McGovern was not always appreciated by some Derby supporters, probably because of his ungainly running style, but he was held in extremely high regard by his teammates. The two-man midfield that Clough decided to employ at the beginning of the season meant that he and Gemmill would often be outnumbered by the opposition. Undeterred, both of them gave it their best shot with McGovern even popping up with the occasional goal.

Not that Brian Clough was too enamoured with him when a sloppy back pass was seized upon by Arsenal's Ray Kennedy in the FA Cup 5th Round second replay on Leicester City's Filbert Street ground before going on to score what turned out to be the only goal of the game. It was an uncharacteristic mistake by the midfielder which would have destroyed some footballers but he quickly bounced back with a series of splendid performances.

A lot of McGovern's work tended to go unnoticed, particularly the way he disrupted the opposition's midfield, and his passing, although not spectacular, was invariably accurate and precise.

Despite his unstinting efforts in midfield, the highlight of his fine season was surely the winning goal against Liverpool at the beginning of May, which as it turned out, clinched the title for Derby. Surely, even his biggest critics couldn't have failed to notice that.

Archie Gemmill

Archie Gemmill had initially taken time to settle into the team after being signed to replace the popular Willie Carlin in September 1970 but once he did it became obvious why Clough had been so keen to acquire his signature. He was absolutely magnificent throughout the 1971-72 season. Not only did he add pace to the midfield his will-to-win rubbed off on everyone.

Gemmill who played 40 League games and was an ever-present in the Football League Cup and the FA Cup, was by now a firm favourite with supporters. Once he was in possession he was difficult to shake off the ball, partly because of his body strength, and he particularly enjoyed running through defences with the ball, allowing teammates the time to get into position to receive a pass. In fact, his passing had improved out of all recognition too which must have been noted by Tommy Docherty because by now he was an integral part of the Scottish international side too.

Although Gemmill only scored three goals in 50 League and Cup appearances, his fine effort against Chelsea at the Baseball Ground on New Year's Day turned out to be the match winner and, coming shortly after the dispiriting 3-0 defeat at Elland Road, it was a particularly important one. But surely his proudest moment must have been collecting the First Division trophy in May in the enforced absence of skipper Roy McFarland.

Kevin Hector

Although Kevin Hector made a massive contribution to the team and was one of the two ever-presents in the side, he didn't have one of his most productive campaigns in terms of goals. For the third season in a row a player who eventually ended his outstanding career with Derby as the club's second highest marksman of all time didn't finish as the top goal scorer.

He began the with a flurry in August and early September with four goals in seven games and ended the campaign with another four including the winner against Ipswich but in between he hit a barren patch and in one period scored just twice in 18 League games.

Not that Hector's teammates or Rams' supporters were complaining. By now Clough was employing him in a slightly more withdrawn role than earlier in his career and occasionally in a wider position too. It was bound to affect his goal tally but he more than made up for his relatively low return with tireless running and accurate passing, laying on numerous goals for his appreciative colleagues.

Hector's ball control, particularly while running at speed, was exceptional. Although there were plenty of defenders who would have loved to give him a kicking they usually found it impossible to get close enough, even at the Baseball Ground where he had the knack of gliding along the muddy surface and leaving less nimble opponents bogged down.

By now Kevin Hector had become the 'King' as far as many supporters were concerned and he was to reign for a few more seasons yet. He had already been selected to represent the Football League and he turned out for them a second time in September 1971. Surprisingly, it would be another two years before Sir Alf Ramsey awarded him his full England cap and by then he was back in his best form in front of goal. Hector eventually finished up with 201 goals for Derby, a total bettered only by Steve Bloomer, and it is unlikely that his 589 appearances for the club will ever be equalled. Forty years later with Hector's reputation so high it seems astonishing that Clough and Taylor had been looking at ways of replacing him.

John O'Hare

It took some Derby County supporters a long time to appreciate the qualities of centre-forward John O'Hare but surely even the most sceptical were converted by the end of the 1971-72 season. Brian Clough never had any doubts though and neither did his colleagues who were well aware of his importance to the team. Scotland manager Tommy Docherty was a big fan too and by now he was back in the national side on a regular basis.

O'Hare's 13 goals in 40 games made him Derby's highest goal scorer from open play that season, just ahead of Hector, but it was his skill at holding on to the ball while being battered and harried by defenders before laying off a pass to a colleague that marked him out as something special. He was immensely brave and although he had no great pace he more made up for that with his positional play and acute football brain.

Just three goals in the first 13 League games may have been less than he would have liked but his outstanding effort in the 2-1 victory over title holders Arsenal in October was one of the highlights of his season. But even that one was surpassed by his opener in the crucial 2-0 win against Leeds at the Baseball Ground at the beginning of April when he headed Alan Durban's cross past 'keeper Sprake with Jack Charlton floundering. Like many other First Division centre-halves, Charlton had found it impossible to cope with O'Hare who had to put up with some particularly rough treatment throughout most of the season.

Alan Hinton

If ever there was any doubt about Alan Hinton's importance in Brian Clough's side it was well and truly dispelled by the end of the 1971-72 season. Not only was he top scorer with 15 League goals plus another two in the League Cup, including eight from penalties, he laid on many more thanks to his uncanny ability to cross a dangerous ball with great accuracy from open play, free-kicks and corners.

Hinton could consider himself fortunate that in Clough he had a manager who was intelligent and shrewd enough to allow him to concentrate on his strengths and not worry too much about any weaknesses. Some accused the winger of lacking courage because of his unwillingness to tackle back and fight for the ball in midfield. But as Clough once said, Hinton's courage lay in taking on hard-tackling full-backs in one-to-one situations and a willingness to take vital penalty kicks under severe pressure.

Hinton might not have scored as many spectacular goals as in previous seasons but by now he had developed the knack of being in the right place at the right time in the penalty area to seize on opportunities in front of goal and he was just as likely to score with his left foot as his right. Although his best crosses tended to come from the left he took his penalties with his right foot, which led many to wonder which was the stronger.

By now his penalty taking had become legendary. Never a one-trick pony from the spot, he had the ability to hit the back of the net from 12 yards in a variety of ways so there wasn't much point in 'keepers studying television footage of his spot-kicks.

Unfortunately, the England manager who had been a full-back himself, had already gained a reputation for picking teams totally devoid of traditional wingers, so Hinton's chances of adding to the England cap that he had won early in his career with Wolves were virtually non-existent. Maybe England's loss was Derby's gain.

Terry Hennessey

Terry Hennessey's season was badly disrupted by injury, which restricted his League appearances to 18 including one as a substitute. A superb player on his day, the Welsh international had played extremely well in pre-season and seemed certain to have a major part to play as the new campaign approached.

With Roy McFarland out of contention early on while recovering from the after-effects of flu, Hennessey's place in the side was more or less assured anyway at that stage. Although he performed creditably in the first three games, two of which were won and the other drawn, McFarland returned as an automatic choice at centre-half and once the manager had decided to add Durban to his line-up, Hennessey's position in the side became less certain.

He had a run in the team during November and most of December playing alongside McFarland and Todd. Occasionally the manager opted to employ him as a defensive midfielder but his League appearances after the turn of the year were restricted to just three starts and the one as a substitute in the defeat at Maine Road in April.

Frank Wignall

Striker Frank Wignall had been signed in February 1969 to add impetus to the promotion campaign by giving Clough a different option up front. Although his appearances during the first two seasons in the top flight had been spasmodic he had provided useful cover in the event of injury to Hector or O'Hare.

During the pre-season tour to Germany and Holland Clough began to experiment with a three-man strike force plus winger Hinton with Wignall playing up front alongside O'Hare and a slightly withdrawn Hector. It seemed to be working so well that the manager continued with the same formation in the early League matches.

By the beginning of September Wignall was Derby's leading goal scorer with four goals in seven appearances. Unfortunately the Rams overall goal tally was too low and the two-man midfield of McGovern and Gemmill was being outnumbered by the opposition. Into the side came Durban who was always likely to pop up with a goal and out went the unlucky Wignall.

From then on there was no place for him and a few weeks later he moved on to Mansfield Town Nevertheless, his five goals in 11 League appearances were a valuable contribution.

Steve Powell

When 16-year-old Steve Powell made his first team debut against Stoke in the Texaco Cup in October 1971 he became the youngest first team player in the club's history. A few days later the son of Derby County legend Tommy Powell came on as a substitute in the First Division match at home to Arsenal and the following Saturday he found himself in Clough's starting XI away at Nottingham Forest. Unfazed by the occasion, Steve put in a fine performance in the 2-0 victory.

Breaking into such a successful side on a regular basis was bound to be difficult and it wasn't until the crucial encounter with Liverpool in the last match of the season that he made his next appearance. Powell will forever be remembered for his wonderful performance on that Monday evening at the beginning of May as Webster's replacement. Afterwards, he went on to have a fine career with the Rams making a total of 409 starts (three more than his illustrious father) stretching over 14 seasons.

Tony Bailey

Burton upon Trent born Tony Bailey made one First Division appearance for Derby. Unfortunately for Tony, that brief 90 minutes of fame came at Elland Road on a day that Derby were completely outplayed in a 3-0 defeat against a Leeds outfit in top form. Todd and Durban were unavailable through injury and with Hennessey already in the side the manager gave Bailey the nod. Although he didn't let himself down it was too much to expect him to shine in that company.

He did make another three appearances during the season They were in the Texaco Cup, firstly away at Dundee United in Round One, then as a substitute at home to Stoke in Round Two and finally in the 3-2 victory at Newcastle United's St James' Park in front of a massive crowd which went into extra-time. I think most Derby County wannabes would settle for that.

The Texaco Boys

The first-team appearances of six other Derby County players in the 1971-72 season were restricted to the Texaco Cup. They were defenders Peter Daniel and Alan Lewis, midfielder Tony Parry, along with three young strikers, Barry Butlin, Jeff Bourne and new signing Roger Davies.

Daniel, who had been a professional with the Rams since 1964, was unlucky not to get an opportunity to shine in the League, the FA Cup or the League Cup. He had been playing particularly well for the reserve side so his five appearances in the Texaco Cup were probably some consolation but as it turned out later, there was no need for him to be too upset. It would all come right for him in the 1974-75 campaign under manager Dave Mackay when he was voted Player of the Season as the Rams went on to lift the title for the second time.

Left-back Alan Lewis who had to be content with a single appearance in the sponsored tournament (the 3-2 victory at home to Stoke), played in a couple of First Division matches for Derby the following season before being loaned out to Peterborough in 1974 and then on to Brighton on a permanent basis.

Midfielder Tony Parry who hailed from Burton had already enjoyed six seasons at Hartlepool where he had become a favourite with supporters before joining the Rams. He went on to make four starts with the club the following season plus another two as a substitute before eventually ending his career with Gresley Rovers.

Barry Butlin had been with Derby since 1967 but had only made a handful of appearances for the first team. Clough decided to select him for three Texaco Cup games after he had turned in some good performances for the reserves and he found the net in the 3-2 defeat at Dundee United.

He was to make one more League appearance for the Rams but unfortunately it was in the 4-0 thumping by Manchester City in November 1972. Days later he moved on to Luton and his time at Kenilworth Road turned out be the next stage in a successful career which included three years at Nottingham Forest before eventually ending up at Sheffield United,

Jeff Bourne who had joined Derby from local club Linton United in January 1969 played in the 6-2 win against Dundee United in the Texaco Cup and although six different players found the back of the net, Bourne wasn't one of them. Later he went on to enjoy a productive career with the Rams making a total of 72 appearances including 24 as a substitute, scoring a respectable 14 goals.

Bourne's best times with Derby came under manager Dave Mackay between 1974 and 1976 and he was particularly prominent in the 1974-75 UEFA Cup campaign scoring two goals against Velez Mostar at the Baseball Ground. He joined Dallas Cowboys on loan in 1976 before being transferred to Crystal Palace the following March.

Peter Taylor spotted Roger Davies playing for non-League Worcester City and shortly afterwards Brian Clough signed him for a record £14,000 in August 1971. He scored on his debut in the Texaco Final against Airdrieonians and went on to have an excellent career with the club. He broke into Clough's League side the following season, vying with O'Hare for the centre-forward position, and in February 1973 he hit the headlines by scoring a hat-trick in the famous 5-3 FA Cup victory against Spurs at White Hart Lane.

Davies won England Under 23 honours when he came on as a substitute for Bob Latchford against Scotland in March 1974. He was an integral part of Derby's second title winning campaign playing in all but three League games and scoring 12 goals. He was transferred to Club Brugge KV for a transfer fee of £135,000 in 1976 and after a particularly successful time in Belgium returned to England to play for Leicester City before embarking on a career in the States. A second spell with Derby in 1979 was less productive.

Clough and Taylor

There have been more books written about Brian Clough than any other manager in the history of the game although he would be the first to say that despite their disagreements and eventual falling out he couldn't have achieved what he did with Peter Taylor.

Of course there have been other great football managers in England over the last 40 years such as Liverpool's Bill Shankly and Bob Paisley and more recently Sir Alex Ferguson and Arsène Wenger but it is unlikely that any of them could have equalled, let alone surpassed, what Clough did with the resources at his disposal at Derby and later at Nottingham Forest.

Maybe Roy Keane, who played under Clough for Forest between 1990 and 1993 before moving to Old Trafford to spend 12 full seasons under Ferguson followed by a short period at Celtic summed up his status in the game better than most when he said recently that Brian Clough was by far the best manager he had played for. That says it all.

Appearances

	League	FA Cup	League Cup	Texaco Cup	Total
Boulton	42	5	2	8	57
Hector	42	5	2	6	55
Robson	41	5	2	6	54
Todd	40	5	2	6	53
Hinton	38	5	2	8	53
O'Hare	40	5	2	5	52
Gemmill	40	5	2	3	50
McGovern	39 (1)	5	1	6	51 (1)
Webster	38	5	2	5	50
McFarland	38	5	2	2	47
Durban	31	5	1	4	41
Hennessey	17 (1)	0 (1)	0	8	25 (1)
Wignall	10 (1)	0	2	3	15 (1)
Walker	3 (3)	0	0	2 (2)	5 (5)
Powell	2 (1)	0 (1)	0	2	4 (2)
Bailey	1	0	0	2 (1)	3 (1)

Appearances of the following players were restricted to the Texaco Cup

Daniel   5

Butlin   3

Davies   1

Bourne   1

Parry   1

Lewis   1

Goalscorers

	League	FA Cup	League Cup	Texaco Cup	Total
O'Hare	13			4	17
Hinton	15	2		3	20
Hector	12	3		2	17
Durban	6	4		1	11
Wignall	5			1	6
McGovern	3			1	4
McFarland	4				4
Robson	2	1		1	4
Gemmill	3				3
Todd	2			1	3
Walker	1			2	3
Webster	1				1
Butlin				1	1
Davies				1	1
Own-goals	2				2
Total	69	10	0	18	97

What Happened Next?

Derby County supporters may have been basking in glory for a few weeks after their heroes had lifted the First Division trophy but Clough and Taylor were already looking forward to the next season. One thing was certain, if they were going to make an impact in the European Cup and retain their First Division title they would have to strengthen and enlarge the squad.

Clough had often made it clear that he would never be completely satisfied and would always strive to improve the quality of players under his command. 'If I can find a better centre-half than McFarland then I'll be after him,' he once said. He couldn't. Although there some promising young players coming through such as Steve Powell, Jeff Bourne and Roger Davies, further additions would almost certainly be necessary to cope with the extra demands of Europe and they might not always be as lucky with injuries as they had been so far.

Clough had been keeping tabs on two Leicester City players, left-back David Nish and midfielder Graham Cross and it had recently become known that they might be available for the right price.

When the new season got underway on Saturday 12 August 1972 with an away match at Southampton, Derby's squad was virtually unchanged and the line-up that afternoon was exactly the same as it had been for much of the previous season. A few days later the manager broke the British transfer record by paying £225,000 for the classy Nish but Cross eventually decided to stay at Filbert Street, much to Clough's irritation.

Surprisingly, instead of increasing the size of his squad with more competition for places, the manager decided to let Robson move on and he was transferred to Aston Villa in December but not until he had helped the Rams overwhelm Benfica 3-0 in the first leg of a European Cup tie at the Baseball Ground. It was a shame to see the side beginning to break up, just as it had earlier when Green, Mackay and Carlin had left the club, but change was inevitable if the Rams were going to move forward.

Derby had a poor start to the new season in the First Division and were languishing in the bottom half of the table when FK Zeljeznicar Sarajevo arrived for a European Cup First Round tie at the Baseball Ground on 13 September 1972. The Rams won 2-0 and a fortnight later they beat their Yugoslav opponents 2-1 in the return fixture, going through 4-1 on aggregate. The European adventure had started well and the following April Clough's men were travelling to Turin to take on Juventus in the first leg of the semi-final after overcoming Benfica and Spartak Trnava of Czechoslovakia on the way.

Although they were denied a place in the final by the Italian giants in dubious circumstances, they had done themselves and the country proud in a competition that was restricted to champions of their respective Leagues. By now any talk that they had won the League title in 1972 by default was long gone.

Clough had signed 'keeper Graham Moseley from Blackburn Rovers in September 1971 and although he had done extremely well in the reserves, Boulton's place in the side had not looked under threat. Very little changed in the 1972-73 season and thanks to his sheer consistency the long serving 'keeper missed just a couple of League games.

Webster was now in his 13th season. He had been an important player but he couldn't go on forever. An injury against Chelsea in August allowed the immensely promising Steve Powell to come into the side and with Webster's recovery taking longer than expected he kept his place until the beginning of November. It wasn't until three seasons later that Rod Thomas was recruited from Swindon to challenge and eventually take over from the Belper born stalwart.

McGovern and Gemmill continued to play regularly in midfield throughout most of the 1972-73 season but Durban's appearances were restricted to 11 starts and seven as a substitute. Henry Newton was already being tipped as his eventual successor but Forest wouldn't allow that to happen and Clough had to wait another year to sign him after he had moved from the City Ground to Everton.

Up front, although O'Hare was still playing well he wasn't scoring as regularly as the manager would have liked and half way through the season Clough opted to switch him into midfield and give Roger Davies his chance. It worked. Before long Davies was posing a threat to the best defences in the country, as his 13 goals in 24 League and Cup games proved and O'Hare continued to make a valuable contribution in midfield.

When the season had begun there were hopes that Kevin Hector might return to his best form in front of goal. Although his tally in the League turned out to be only marginally better than the previous season, he rattled in another five goals in the FA Cup plus four more in the European Cup making a total of 23 altogether.

Alan Hinton began the new campaign with a goal in the first League match and once he returned to the side at the beginning of September after missing four games through injury he went on to score an impressive 13 goals in 27 League games.

Although supporters had to be content with seventh place in the First Division at the end of the season they had been thrilled to see their side doing so well in the European Cup. Clough's side had enjoyed an extended run in the FA Cup too, reaching the quarter-final stage before losing narrowly at home to Leeds.

Unfortunately, behind the scenes relationships between the management and the board were worsening and it wouldn't be long before things came to a head.

Forty Years On

The 1971-72 Season in Retrospect

Derby County's feat of lifting the First Division title at the end of the 1971-72 season seemed remarkable at the time. Forty years later it seems even more astonishing, particularly considering the limited resources available to the manager, the strength of the opposition and what eventually turned out to be insurmountable problems behind the scenes at the Baseball Ground.

Football in England was already being dominated by the big city clubs such as Arsenal, Leeds United, Liverpool, Everton, along with the two Manchester sides. The last so-called provincial club to lift the trophy had been Alf Ramsey's Ipswich Town in 1962. What Derby County achieved under Brian Clough and Peter Taylor would be inconceivable today.

At a time when Premier League squads have to be restricted to 25 players, most of which are being rotated in order to keep fresh, it seems even more astonishing that Derby County were able to win the title with a core of only 13 recognised first team players at the beginning of the season which was reduced to 12 when Clough decided to allow Wignall to move on in December. And one of those, Hennessey, was being troubled with knee and tendon injuries for most of the campaign. Even more remarkable, the same group of players turned out in all seven League Cup and FA Cup ties too as well as most of Texaco Cup matches.

How good were they?

Although Brian Clough had assembled an extremely talented squad of players, much of their success was built on an outstanding team spirit, discipline and a willingness to play week-in, week-out, occasionally when not fully fit.

They were not a team of world famous superstars, in fact only three of the 13 recognised first team players were regular internationals when the 1971-72 season began. McFarland had cemented his place in Ramsey's England side, O'Hare was playing regularly for Scotland and Durban, who had already won 22 caps for Wales, was about to turn out in five more international matches

Of the others, Gemmill had played just once for Scotland, Hennessey had been selected three times for Wales and Hinton had been awarded his single England cap while playing for Wolves much earlier in his career. In the meantime, although Todd was being talked of as the next Bobby Moore, he was still on the fringe of the England squad. Boulton and Webster, despite their reputation for reliability and consistency, never received international recognition, Robson had to make do with a handful of England Under-23 appearances and McGovern was yet to win full international honours for Scotland.

Forty years later, England are still searching for a centre-half as accomplished as Roy McFarland and although Colin Todd's international career was not as extensive as it should have been, their partnership in central defensive has only rarely been matched since. In fact McFarland has been judged by no less than respected football writer David Miller as second only to Bobby Moore in the last half century.

Rather like Boulton and Webster, Kevin Hector was unlucky to be around when competition for places in the England set-up was particularly fierce. He was extremely unlucky to make just a couple of substitute appearances for his country. Far worse strikers have played for England since. As for Gemmill, McGovern and O'Hare, all three would be regulars into today's Scotland side, as would Durban and a fit Hennessey for Wales.

Over the years most successful teams have had at least one prolific striker scoring a minimum of 20 League goals. Derby were an exception that season. Hinton was the top scorer with just 15 in the League, including eight from the spot, followed by O'Hare and Hector with 13 and 12 respectively. But with Wignall's five goals early on and the midfielders chipping in (particularly Durban) plus a handful from McFarland, Todd, Webster and Robson, the overall goal tally was just about enough.

Comparing teams and players from different eras is always fraught with danger but it is intriguing to speculate how Derby's 1971-72 side would perform today. The vast improvement in playing surfaces and the lighter ball would certainly suit their style of play and the referees' clamp down on the sort of thuggery that was all too prevalent 40 years ago would go in their favour too. The faster pace of football today would suit them too because there was plenty of pace in the side. As for the three scourges of the modern game, diving, shirt pulling and feigning injury, Clough would never allow his players to indulge in any of that nonsense and neither would they want to.

The Opposition

What made lifting the First Division trophy so special was that Clough's tiny squad had to finish above at least three exceptionally strong outfits to do so. Before the season began, most bookies had marked Leeds United as favourites for the title. Manager Don Revie had put together a formidable squad of players. Not only were most of them exceptionally skilful, they could be intimidating too with a mean streak, not averse to engaging in gamesmanship (or even worse) and were packed with winners. Even their detractors (and there were plenty of those) had to agree that they were a great side.

Arguably, their only weakness was in goal where Gary Sprake was liable to drop the occasional clanger but with Charlton and Hunter in defence, Bremner and Giles bossing the midfield, Lorimer and Gray on the wings and Clarke and Jones up front, the side was packed with top class internationals and it had depth too. Veteran centre-half Jack Charlton might have been slightly past his best but Revie had Terry Yorath and the versatile Paul Madeley available too. By then the rivalry between Derby and Leeds was already intense and would become increasingly bitter later as the dislike between the respective managers escalated.

Liverpool were obviously going to be strong contenders as well. Shankly's squad, all the way from England 'keeper Ray Clemence to left winger Peter Thompson, was full of stars. Full-backs Lawler and Lindsay were among the best in the land, Tommy Smith and Larry Lloyd formed a fearsome central defensive duo and up front there was the Keegan/Toshack partnership. Emlyn Hughes was approaching his peak and there were other top class players such as to Steve Heighway and Ian Callaghan.

As for the current titleholders Arsenal who had also won the FA Cup the previous season, there was no reason why they shouldn't be in the mix again. Bob Wilson was a fine 'keeper, Pat Rice and Bob McNab were competent full-backs and with the likes of McLintock, Storey and Simpson in the side, they were unlikely to concede many goals. Alan Ball had been signed from Everton and he was bound to find his best form before long. John Radford and Ray Kennedy formed a dangerous pairing up front and George Armstrong was a tricky winger. Then there was the talented George Graham as well as a young star in the making, Charlie George.

Manchester City with so many top class players all the way from 'keeper Joe Corrigan and full back Tony Book up to the likes of Colin Bell, Francis Lee and Mike Summerbee would almost certainly be in with shout and although there were signs that things were not quite right at Old Trafford it would be dangerous to dismiss United as long as Charlton, Law and Best could do the business.

So it was particularly surprising to see Sheffield United leading the table early on in the season. Manchester United also began well but the Yorkshire side were never strong enough to stay at the top and by the turn of the year it was becoming apparent that Busby's ageing side was in decline and their problems were exacerbated by the behaviour of the increasingly errant George Best. Three seasons later, of course, they were relegated to the Second Division.

Leeds United who had been widely tipped before the season began were, as expected, in contention all the way through as were Liverpool and Manchester City, both of whom like Derby never dropped out of the top six. Titleholders Arsenal, on the other hand, despite a fine run of results in the middle of the season never really threatened to hang on to their First Division title.

Behind the scenes

In hindsight Derby's success that season seems even more remarkable considering the deteriorating relations between Brian Clough and chairman Sam Longson. It has been shown many times since that some sort of rapport between the manager and his chairman is absolutely crucial but here they were, barely on speaking terms at times and, as it turned out, the whole saga was doomed to end in bitter recriminations.

Although it was another two years before Clough and Taylor left the club, it was already becoming increasingly clear as the season progressed that relationships between the management team and various members of the board were coming under strain. Some had been unhappy about the way Clough had signed Colin Todd for a huge transfer fee the previous February without much involvement of the chairman or the board. They were becoming increasingly concerned about some of his controversial comments in the media too which they found embarrassing.

All the same, at the beginning of the season Longson and Clough seemed to be getting on reasonably well although maybe not quite as friendly as they had been in earlier years when Longson apparently carried a photo of his charismatic manager in his wallet. The chairman seemed to be getting increasingly uncomfortable about Clough's influence across the whole club and so did some of the other board members. Maybe they were jealous of his high profile too. Sometimes it seemed that they would have been far happier trundling along in the Second Division with a manager they could dominate rather than having to deal with strong-minded individuals such as Clough and Taylor.

There were mutterings about Clough's political leanings too, particularly as he wasn't shy about airing them in public and for a while it seemed that he might even be tempted to go into politics, maybe as a labour Member of Parliament. Worse still, the manager was getting all the publicity and most of the credit, Longson was getting very little of either and outsiders were wondering who was running the club, the manager or the directors.

In the meantime Clough had already shown some impatience and this had been noted by others. It had been rumoured that Birmingham City and Coventry City fancied tempting him away from the Baseball Ground and even that Manchester United had been interested in the possibility of him taking over from Sir Matt Busby. The Greek national side had been looking for a head coach too.

The situation was not helped by what became known as the Ian Storey-Moore fiasco. The high-scoring Nottingham Forest winger wanted to get away from the City Ground and in the end they decided to let him go and invited offers for him. A number of clubs including Manchester City and Everton did just that followed by Manchester United. By this time the transfer fee had risen to around £200,000 before, at last, Clough made his move. Forest, somewhat reluctantly, allowed Derby to make an approach, a fee was agreed as were personal terms with the player which were better than those offered by United.

Storey-Moore signed the necessary forms and with what seemed the formality of Forest officials signing too, he was paraded in front of supporters at a packed Baseball Ground prior to the kick-off for the Wolves match on Saturday 4 March. Later it became clear that Forest had not officially sanctioned the move. The player, apparently with the encouragement of his wife, then changed his mind and joined United instead.

Not surprisingly, Derby were found guilty of breaching Football League regulations and were fined £5,000, warned about the way they conducted future transfers and left with egg on their respective faces. Clough was bitterly disappointed but the directors were furious and relationships that were already strained were close to breaking point. Despite the furore caused by the whole affair, the players, to their credit, carried on as if nothing had happened.

The following week Derby beat Spurs 1-0 at White Hart Lane and it was looking as though Derby were in with a chance of lifting the title. A few days earlier Derrick Robbins, the Coventry City chairman, had spoken to Clough about taking over at Highfield Road after getting permission from an increasingly unhappy Sam Longson but the manager, who had managed to get an increase in his salary, decided to turn down their approach and stay with the club.

Derby, of course, had a chance of lifting the title, Coventry, although ambitious, were a million miles away from achieving that so Clough decided to see it through at the Baseball Ground. At least for the time being.

The Fans

Although the overwhelming majority of supporters were thrilled with what Clough and Taylor were achieving at the Baseball Ground, unfortunately there was a small minority who seemed intent on criticising individual players with the hardworking McGovern getting the brunt of it, much to Clough's exasperation. But Durban, O'Hare and even top scorer Hinton were not immune either although Hector, who had endured a barren patch in terms of goals in mid-season, remained a firm favourite with fans.

The manager wasn't altogether happy with attendances at the Baseball Ground either. Although the average of just over 33,000 for League matches was around 2,000 higher than that for the previous season, it was well down on that of just under 36,000 in the 1969-70 campaign; Derby's first back in the top flight.

He was particularly upset when only 26,738 turned up for the match against Ipswich Town in late March. Derby were riding high in second place behind leaders Manchester City at the time and four days earlier they had thrashed Leicester City 3 0 at the Baseball Ground for their fourth win a row. The attendance at the Leicester match had been over 34,000, which meant that around 7,000 supporters who had watched that game had decided not to turn up for the Ipswich match.

On a happier note, Derby County and their attractive style of football attracted extremely large attendances on their travels. Only Leeds and Manchester United attracted bigger crowds for their away matches. Derby's average of around 35,500 which was significantly higher than that of reigning double holders Arsenal and slightly above Liverpool's too.

The scourge of football hooliganism was becoming a problem by the early 1970s but, thankfully, Rams' fans were generally regarded as among the best behaved and any trouble at the Baseball Ground or its environs was usually attributed to the opposition fans with Manchester United among most troublesome.

The Media

By now Brian Clough had become a firm favourite with journalists. He never left them short of copy and they loved his quotes. Unfortunately, although the majority of the more intelligent and fair-minded journalists were prepared to give Derby the credit they deserved for winning the First Division title, some were less than complimentary or even churlish at times. Their main problem seemed to be was that Derby was situated in the unfashionable East Midlands.

A few writers based in the capital made it quite clear that they would have been far happier had Arsenal retained the trophy but except for a short period at the turn of the year when they threatened to break into the top three, the Gunners had never been in the running.

Others seemed particularly peeved that Leeds had buckled at the final hurdle after being forced to play their final League game two days after beating Arsenal in the Cup Final. With Derby finishing their season before Leeds and Liverpool had played their final games, others even went as far as saying that Derby had won the title 'by default'. That was not only insulting, it was ludicrous too. Derby were champions because they won more points from their 42 matches than any of their competitors. It was as simple as that. They had also beaten Leeds and Liverpool when it really mattered, in April and May.

Desmond Hackett of the Daily Express, famous for threatening to eat his bowler hat if ever he was proved wrong, wrote, 'Leeds were deprived of the double they so richly deserved. I say deprived', he added, 'because robbed is such a dirty word'.

Some journalists thought that the muddy Baseball Ground had given Derby an unfair advantage. In fact, it was probably the other way round because Clough's players had to cope with the energy-sapping surface for weeks on end whereas opposition sides only had to endure it once. The accusation was misleading anyway because Derby won more away games than any other club in the First Division and their home record was actually inferior to that of Leeds and Liverpool.

Even Derby's reputation for sportsmanship hadn't been enough to win over some observers. It was common knowledge that referees loved officiating in their matches because they knew there would be no back-chat from Clough's players. There were no out-and-out destroyers in his side either so refs knew that they wouldn't be brandishing very many yellow cards let alone reds. In fact not a single player was sent off all season. McFarland and Todd could tackle as fiercely as anyone in the First Division but their methods were far removed from those of Leeds United's Norman 'Bite your legs' Hunter, Chelsea's 'Chopper' Harris, Liverpool hard man Tommy Smith or Peter Storey, the Arsenal destroyer.

Fortunately in Brian Clough, Derby had a manager who was more than a match for most journalists. He had the last laugh the following season too when his side confounded all the pessimists by reaching the semi-final stage of the European Cup before going out to Juventus in extremely dubious circumstances.

On the other hand, the vast majority of managers from rival clubs were invariably complimentary about the Rams and their style of play. Bill Shankly and even Don Revie, both of whom had come so close to pipping Clough at the post, were quick to praise Derby. After Liverpool's goalless draw at Highbury in their crucial last match of the season Shankly had said, 'My only consolation for losing the Championship is that the best team we have played this season won the League', before adding, 'they are also the most entertaining'. Shortly after Wolves had beaten Leeds at Molyneux in a controversial match the same night that ruined his side's hopes, Revie apparently was quoted as saying, 'I am very pleased for Derby, they will make worthy champions'.

How do They Compare?

Derby County have enjoyed three extended periods in the top flight since those halcyon days under Clough and Taylor plus a very brief fourth one, which is probably best forgotten. The first began when Dave Mackay took over from Clough in October 1973 and lasted until the end of the 1979-80 season by which time Colin Addison was in charge. Arthur Cox was the manager for the second spell, which began in 1987 and lasted until the end of the 1990-91 season and a few years after that Derby were playing in the top flight again with Jim Smith in charge.

Dave Mackay's squad, although built on the one that Clough and Taylor left behind, was strengthened by the addition of Rod Thomas, Bruce Rioch and Francis Lee and they won the title for the second time at the end of the 1974-75 season. Mackay was, arguably, the only person who could have succeeded after Clough's acrimonious departure and once the players had settled down after the initial turmoil they began to perform splendidly.

Mackay's feat in winning the title was a magnificent achievement and maybe doesn't get the praise it deserves. In contrast to Clough's team, which was built on a strong defence, a disciplined midfield and a two man strike force plus a goal-scoring winger, Mackay's side were far more cavalier in their approach. If the opposition scored two goals, then Derby would more than likely get three.

Which was the better of the two sides is matter of opinion. The big difference was that Clough started with a relatively weak group of players whereas Mackay had plenty to build on. Shortly after winning the title Mackay signed Charlie George from Arsenal to strengthen his squad further, followed by Burnley's Welsh international winger Leighton James. Derby went into decline after Mackay left the club in November 1977 after failing to get a vote of confidence from the directors. A series of managers, including Tommy Docherty, failed to turn things round and Derby were relegated in 1980.

After that, it wasn't until the 1987-88 season that the club was playing in the top flight. By then Arthur Cox had masterminded successive promotions from the Third Division to the First and his excellent side finished fifth at the end of the 1988-89 campaign. It was the club's highest position since 1976.

Although nowhere near as successful as Clough's Championship winning team (or Mackay's), Cox's side was built on similar principles to Clough's, hard work and discipline and an indomitable team spirit. By 1987 he had signed a clutch of top class players to give his squad a chance of competing with the best. Peter Shilton had finally arrived at the Baseball Ground along with England international centre-half Mark Wright followed by striker Dean Saunders so the spine of the side was almost as strong as Clough's. Shilton would certainly have found a place in the 1971-72 squad and probably Wright and Saunders too.

Ten years later Jim Smith had assembled another outstanding Derby County side, which finished in ninth place at the end of the 1997-98 season and one position higher a year later. It was built around a strong backbone too. Mart Poom was a top class 'keeper, Laursen and Stimac formed the basis of a mean defence and with the likes of Sturridge and Wanchope up front, there was no shortage of goals. He had put together a well-balanced midfield too which included the likes of Eranio, and (briefly) Asanovic. Although the side was never quite good enough to mount a serious challenge for the title, once again it is intriguing to speculate whether the likes of Poom, Stimac and Eranio would have displaced any of Clough's players.

In 2009 Derby County supporters were invited to select what they considered to be the best player in each position over their 125-year history. Some thought that they might just as well nominate the 11 regulars from the 1971-72 season but in the end seven were selected, Boulton, Webster, McFarland, Durban, Gemmill, Hector and Hinton. Bizarrely Colin Todd, player of the year in 1972, was overlooked, as were O'Hare, McGovern and Robson. But there again, so were Carter and Doherty as well as Charlie George.

After winning the First Division title in May 1972 Brian Clough described the feat as one of the miracles of the twentieth century. All we need now, 12 years into the 21st with Nigel Clough in charge is another one.

Bibliography

Derby Evening Telegraph

Derby County: A Complete Record 1884–1988 Gerald Mortimer (Breedon Books, 1988)

Derby County: The Complete Record Gerald Mortimer (Breedon Books, 2006)

The 1971-72 editions of *The Ram*, Derby County's match day newspaper-style programme

Derby County: Champions of England 1971-72 and 1974-75 Edward Giles (Desert Island Books Ltd, 2005)

Derby County: The Clough Years Michael Cockayne (The Parrs Wood Press, 2003)

Brian Clough, the Biography; Nobody Ever Says Thank You Jonathan Wilson (Orion Books, 2011)

The Life of Brian Tim Crane (Football World, 2004)

The *Rothmans Football Yearbooks* for 1971-72 and 1972-73

ND - #0322 - 270225 - C0 - 234/156/10 - PB - 9781780910772 - Gloss Lamination